Carl Sandburg Home National Historic Site

Geologic Resources Inventory Report

Natural Resource Report NPS/NRSS/GRD/NRR—2012/501

National Park Service
Geologic Resources Division
PO Box 25287
Denver, CO 80225

March 2012

U.S. Department of the Interior
National Park Service
Natural Resource Stewardship and Science
Fort Collins, Colorado

The National Park Service, Natural Resource Stewardship and Science office in Denver, Colorado publishes a range of reports that address natural resource topics of interest and applicability to a broad audience in the National Park Service and others in natural resource management, including scientists, conservation and environmental constituencies, and the public.

The Natural Resource Report Series is used to disseminate high-priority, current natural resource management information with managerial application. The series targets a general, diverse audience, and may contain NPS policy considerations or address sensitive issues of management applicability.

All manuscripts in the series receive the appropriate level of peer review to ensure that the information is scientifically credible, technically accurate, appropriately written for the intended audience, and designed and published in a professional manner. This report received informal peer review by subject-matter experts who were not directly involved in the collection, analysis, or reporting of the data.

Views, statements, findings, conclusions, recommendations, and data in this report do not necessarily reflect views and policies of the National Park Service, U.S. Department of the Interior. Mention of trade names or commercial products does not constitute endorsement or recommendation for use by the U.S. Government.

Printed copies of this report are produced in a limited quantity and they are only available as long as the supply lasts. This report is available from the Geologic Resources Inventory website (http://www.nature.nps.gov/geology/inventory/gre_publications.cfm) and the Natural Resource Publications Management website (http://www.nature.nps.gov/publications/nrpm/).

Please cite this publication as:

NPS 445/113350, March 2012

Contents

List of Figures

List of Tables

Executive Summary

This report accompanies the digital geologic map data for Carl Sandburg Home National Historic Site in North Carolina, produced by the Geologic Resources Division in collaboration with its partners. It contains information relevant to resource management and scientific research. This document incorporates preexisting geologic information and does not include new data or additional fieldwork by the Geologic Resources Division.

In 1945, Pulitzer Prize-winning author and "poet of the people" Carl Sandburg moved from Michigan to a country estate near Flat Rock, North Carolina. Sandburg authored more than a third of his works while living at the estate, called Connemara. The landscape of Connemara, with rock outcrops along the flanks of Glassy Mountain, inspired Sandburg and his family. He spent much time out-of-doors on the grounds of Connemara, his chair remains perched on one of Sandburg's favorite rock outcrops behind the house. Following Sandburg's 1967 death, the property was designated Carl Sandburg Home National Historic Site in 1968 and opened to visitors in 1974.

Geologic processes give rise to the rock formations, mountains, balds, valleys, and ponds that formed the inspirational landscape of the park and surrounding area. In particular, the "balds" or "granitic domes," were focal points for much of the history of the park, and preserve globally-rare habitat.

More than a slice of Appalachian geology, Carl Sandburg Home offers insights into the history of a famous American author, among the mountains surrounding his country home and farm. This history is reflected in the buildings, gardens, and fields found there. It is not surprising, then, that some of the principal geologic issues and concerns pertain to preserving these features.

The following geologic issues, features, and processes were identified at a scoping meeting in 2000 and a follow-up conference call in 2011. They are further described in the respective sections of the report.

- Landscape Preservation. The historic landscape of the park is managed as a cultural resource. Preserving viewsheds, and restoring historic structures and the landscape around them, require balancing the continuous natural processes of erosion and weathering with the demands of increasing local population and urban development. Cultural resource management often requires understanding of natural geologic processes.
- Water-related issues. The park receives more than 1,440 mm (57 in.) of precipitation annually. Water is present in streams, springs, groundwater, ponds, lakes, and wetlands. Unlike rocks such as limestones, the underlying rock types at the park lack the necessary chemical characteristics to buffer acidic rain water. Streamflow, channel morphology, and sediment loads continually fluctuate at the park. These changes affect aquatic and riparian ecosystems. The ponds and lakes

within the park are all anthropogenic, impounded by dams that may need maintenance. Wetlands provide records of paleoconditions and are not well studied within the park.
- Seismicity. Carl Sandburg Home National Historic Site occasionally experiences minor earthquakes. Seismic monitoring data may help determine the frequency of earthquake activity, evaluate earthquake risk, interpret the geologic and tectonic activity of the area, and provide an effective vehicle for public information and education.
- Mass wasting. The relatively wet climate of the eastern U.S., combined with the high slopes of the Balsam Mountains, creates a setting which is susceptible to slumping and landslide problems. Areas with a lack of stabilizing vegetation are particularly susceptible. This is not considered a major issue in the park, although the potential exists.

The rocks present beneath and surrounding Carl Sandburg Home National Historic Site record the evolution of the Appalachian Mountains over hundreds of millions of years. The oldest metamorphic rocks (gneisses, schists, and migmatites) and intrusive igneous rocks exposed in the Blue Ridge and Piedmont physiographic provinces are more than a billion years old. On top of this basement, sandstones, shales, siltstones, carbonates, and quartzites were deposited over hundreds of millions of years as ocean basins opened and closed, the Appalachian Mountains formed, and Pangaea was assembled.

Molten material (now granite) intruded those rocks. As Pangaea was being assembled, large landmasses (terranes) were sutured to the eastern margin of North America during the compression associated with three major tectonic, mountain-building events: the Taconic, Neoacadian, and Alleghany orogenies, ultimately culminating in the formation of the ancient Appalachian Mountains. Metamorphism and igneous activity were associated with these orogenies, as is reflected in the dominant bedrock of the park, the metamorphosed Henderson Augen Gneiss. Ongoing processes of erosion and sedimentation continued during and after each event. The erosion and transport of sediment away from the mountains formed what is now the Coastal Plain.

This report also provides a glossary, which contains explanations of technical, geologic terms. A geologic time scale shows the chronologic arrangement of major geologic events.

Acknowledgements

The Geologic Resources Inventory (GRI) is one of 12 inventories funded by the National Park Service Inventory and Monitoring Program. The GRI is administered by the Geologic Resources Division of the Natural Resource Stewardship and Science Directorate.

The Geologic Resources Division relies heavily on partnerships with institutions such as the U.S. Geological Survey, Colorado State University, state geologic surveys, local museums, and universities in developing GRI products.

Special thanks to: Irene Van Hoff and Jeri DeYoung (both from Carl Sandburg Home NHS) for providing information and images used in the report as well as their thoughtful review comments. Miriam Ferris (Carl Sandburg Home NHS) provided the cover images.

Credits

Author
Trista Thornberry-Ehrlich (Colorado State University)

Review
Mark Carter (U.S. Geological Survey)
Irene Van Hoff (Carl Sandburg Home NHS)
Jeri DeYoung (Carl Sandburg Home NHS)
Jason Kenworthy (NPS Geologic Resources Division)

Editing
Steve Hoffman (Write Science Right)

Digital Geologic Data Production
Philip Reiker (NPS Geologic Resources Division)
Dave Green (Colorado State University)
Stephanie O'Meara (Colorado State University)

Digital Geologic Data Overview Layout Design
Philip Reiker (NPS Geologic Resources Division)

Introduction

The following section briefly describes the National Park Service Geologic Resources Inventory and the regional geologic setting of Carl Sandburg Home National Historic Site.

Purpose of the Geologic Resources Inventory

The Geologic Resources Inventory (GRI) is one of 12 inventories funded by the National Park Service (NPS) Inventory and Monitoring Program. The GRI, administered by the Geologic Resources Division of the Natural Resource Stewardship and Science Directorate, is designed to provide and enhance baseline information available to park managers. The GRI team relies heavily on partnerships with institutions such as the U.S. Geological Survey, Colorado State University, state geologic surveys, local museums, and universities in developing GRI products.

The goals of the GRI are to increase understanding of the geologic processes at work in parks and to provide sound geologic information for use in park decision making. Sound park stewardship requires an understanding of the natural resources and their role in the ecosystem. Park ecosystems are fundamentally shaped by geology. The compilation and use of natural resource information by park managers is called for in section 204 of the National Parks Omnibus Management Act of 1998 and in NPS-75, Natural Resources Inventory and Monitoring Guideline.

To realize these goals, the GRI team is systematically conducting a scoping meeting for each of the 270 identified natural area parks, and providing a park-specific digital geologic map and geologic report. These products support the stewardship of park resources and are designed for nongeoscientists. Scoping meetings bring together park staff and geologic experts to review available geologic maps and discuss specific geologic issues, features, and processes.

The GRI mapping team converts the geologic maps identified for park use at the scoping meeting into digital geologic data in accordance with their Geographic Information Systems (GIS) Data Model. These digital data sets bring an interactive dimension to traditional paper maps. The digital data sets provide geologic data for use in park GIS and facilitate the incorporation of geologic considerations into a wide range of resource management applications. The newest maps contain interactive help files. This geologic report assists park managers in the use of the map and provides an overview of park geology and geologic resource management issues.

For additional information regarding the content of this report and current GRI contact information please refer to the Geologic Resources Inventory website (http://www.nature.nps.gov/geology/inventory/).

History and Establishment of the Park

"What a hell of a baronial estate for an old Socialist."

—Carl Sandburg
Reflecting on his purchase of Connemara in 1945

Carl Sandburg was a renowned poet, biographer, folk singer, lecturer, and winner of two Pulitzer Prizes. His is a reputation of broad and enduring 20th century insight into the circumstances, worth and spirit of the American everyman. It is because of this legacy that Connemara, his home and farm, is managed today by the National Park Service. The National Park Service preserves the 108 ha (264 ac) of historic landscape, including the Sandburg residence, dairy goat barn complex, sheds, trails, rolling pastures, two small lakes, several ponds, gardens, an apple orchard, and mountainside woods (fig. 1).

Tired of harsh northern winters, Carl Sandburg moved to the farm from the family home in Harbert, Michigan in 1945 (Jones 2005). Inspired by the many bedrock outcrops within the estate, the previous owner Ellison Smyth renamed it Connemara, after the rugged landscape of quartzite and schist on Ireland's western coast. The original owner, Christopher G. Memminger, even named the estate Rock Hill, also after the bedrock exposures within the property (Jones 2005). The Sandburg's lived there for 22 years, during which time Sandburg published more than one-third of his literary works and won a Pulitzer Prize in 1950 (his first Pulitzer was awarded in 1941 for his Lincoln biography). Sandburg passed away in 1967. The historic landmark was designated a national historic site on October 17, 1968, and opened to visitors in 1974. More than 89,700 people visited the park in 2011.

The experiences of Carl Sandburg Home National Historic Site extend beyond the history of the Sandburg's. The area's topography and geology are uncommon and complex, as are the flora and fauna that live in the ecosystems supported by the geology and topography.

Park Setting

The site is located in the southern Appalachian Mountains of North Carolina, 64 km (40 mi) southeast of Great Smoky Mountains National Park, and 32 km (20 mi) south of Asheville. The park is situated within Henderson County, in the town of Flat Rock—named for the exposures of Henderson Augen Gneiss (geologic map unit Chg) found in the area. Elevation in the park peaks at 848 m (2,783 ft) on the top of Glassy Mountain (also called Big Glassy Mountain). Little Glassy Mountain rises to 677 m (2,220 ft). The park's lowest elevation is 658 m (2,160 ft), along the northern boundary.

The park is located in the Balsam Mountains, which are a subrange of the Great Smoky Mountains (to the northwest) of the Appalachian Mountains. The Balsam Mountains are one of several "backbone" ranges that form right angles to the general northeast-southwest trend of the Appalachians. The Balsam Mountains (also known as the Great Balsam Mountains) consist of two, near-parallel ridge lines trending northwest-southeast from the Great Smoky Mountains to the South Carolina border: the Pisgah Range and the Great Balsam Range. The Pisgah Range is located south of Asheville, North Carolina and extends through Carl Sandburg Home National Historic Site. The Great Balsam Range is located between the towns of Cherokee and Maggie Valley, North Carolina.

The vista from the trail to Glassy Mountain (named for light reflecting off the exposed bedrock), which begins at the Main House, offers a panoramic view of Mount Pisgah and neighboring peaks of the Balsam Mountains. This report includes Mount Pisgah as part of the Balsam Mountains, although there are some inconsistencies regarding names of mountains and ridges in the area (McDaniel 2000).

Physiographic and Geologic Setting

Carl Sandburg Home National Historic Site is within the Inner Piedmont geologic province (fig. 2). Series of northeast-trending groups, or belts, of rocks (called 'lithotectonic terranes') characterize Piedmont geology in the Carolinas. Terranes are bodies of rock, often bounded by faults, that originated elsewhere and, in North Carolina, were added or accreted onto the continent during the continental collision events that ultimately formed the Appalachian Mountains. Before, during, and after accretion, these terranes were affected by varying degrees of metamorphism at different temperatures and pressures. This resulted in the presence of alternating, parallel bands of metamorphosed rock that trend roughly northeast-southwest. They alternate between low-grade (greenschist facies) and high-grade (amphibolite facies) metamorphism (Horton 2008).

This report uses the terrane definitions outlined in Horton et al. (1994), wherein the Carolina terrane (a large component of the "Carolina Zone" of Hibbard et al. 2002) includes rocks traditionally assigned to the Carolina slate belt, Charlotte belt, Kiokee belt, Belair belt, and the layered metasedimentary and metavolcanic rocks of the (informal) Kings Mountain sequence. Piedmont terranes are bounded by numerous faults and large areas of sheared and deformed rocks. Such areas are called 'fault zones' and 'shear zones,' respectively.

Inner Piedmont rocks are sedimentary rocks that were subsequently metamorphosed by high temperatures and pressures associated with Appalachian Mountain-building into schists, gneisses, migmatites, and amphibolites. There were numerous intrusions of molten material, now represented as layers, dikes, and small plutons of granite and granite-like rocks (Goldsmith 1981). The dominant bedrock in the park, the Henderson Augen Gneiss, was metamorphosed by heat and pressure produced during the numerous collisions that uplifted the Appalachian Mountains. The portion of the Inner Piedmont that contains the park is also referred to as the Columbus Promontory. This is an area of Blue Ridge topography and high relief relative to other parts of the Piedmont (Davis 1993). This is likely due to the erosion-resistant bedrock predominantly made up of gneisses—commonly exposed as bedrock balds at Carl Sandburg Home National Historic Site.

The bedrock of the park is mapped as Henderson Augen Gneiss (geologic map unit Chg) that characteristically forms "domes" and other areas of high relief. High precipitation rates within this area of North Carolina weather the bedrock. This tends to produce acidic regolith, because rainfall leaches most of the soluble basic compounds away. Topography within the park is steep and rugged, particularly along the flanks of Big Glassy and Little Glassy mountains, whose slopes may exceed 65% (Hart 1993). The park is within the French Broad River drainage, which drains westward into the Ohio-Mississippi river system. Drainage patterns within the park originate on Big Glassy and Little Glassy mountains, uniting to form Memminger Creek, which leaves the park under Little River Road.

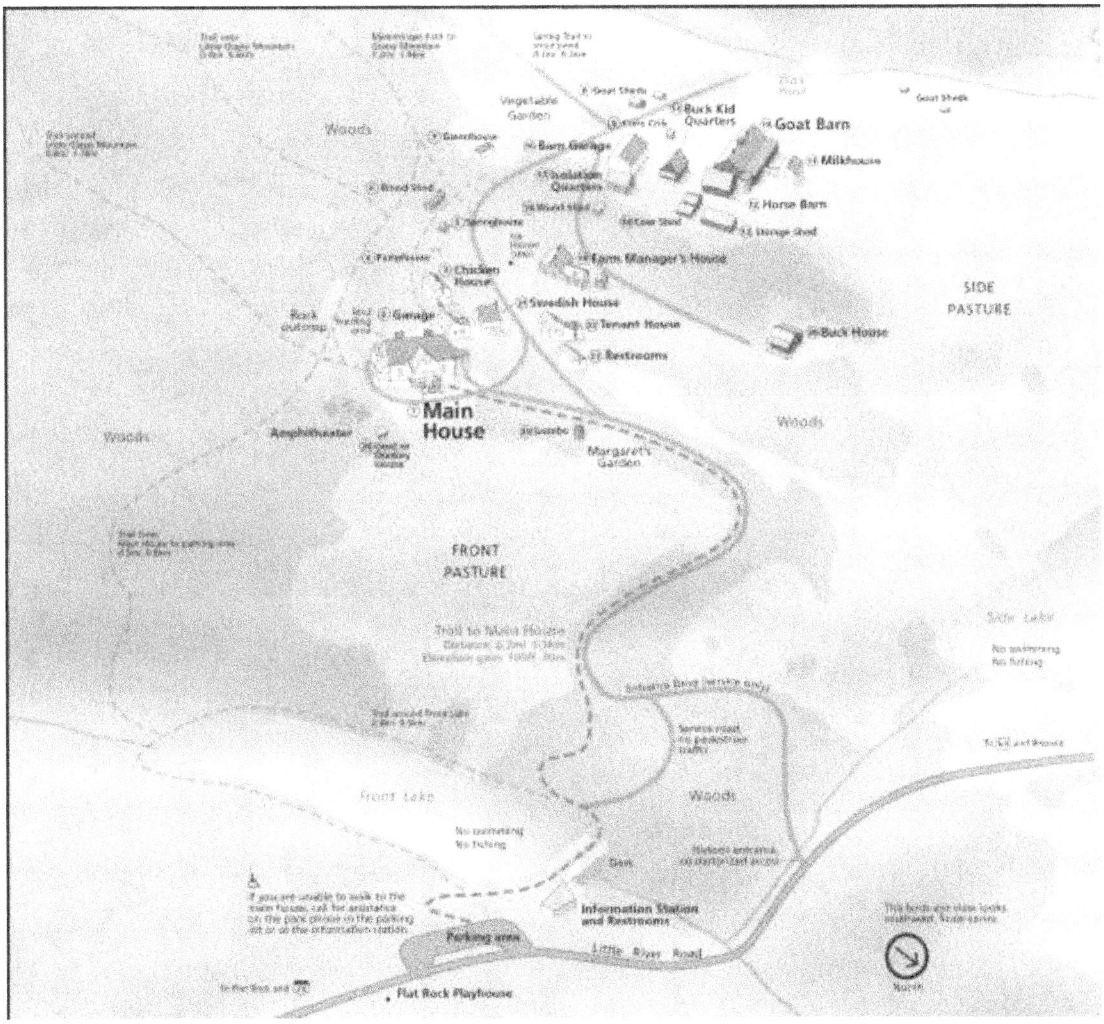

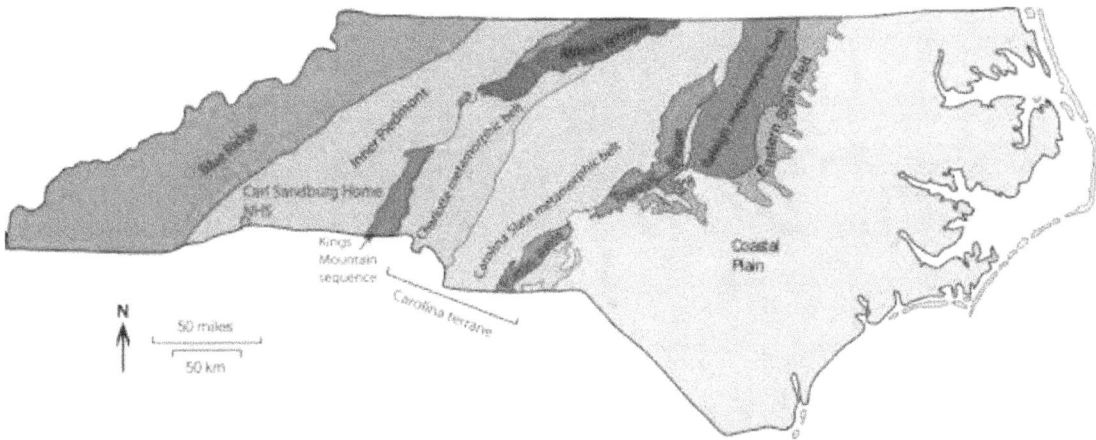

Figure 1. Map of the main house area of Carl Sandburg Home National Historic Site. Note the locations of rock outcrops, and several lakes and ponds within the park. Trails show directions toward topographic features such as Big Glassy Mountain and Little Glassy Mountain. National Park Service graphic. Available online: http://www.nps.gov/hfc/cfm/carto.cfm (accessed 19 January 2012).

Figure 2. Map of the geologic provinces in North Carolina. Note the location of Carl Sandburg Home National Historic Site (green circle) in the Inner Piedmont province. The provinces west of the Coastal Plain were all deformed during the construction of the Appalachian Mountains. The Coastal Plain encompasses generally undeformed sedimentary rocks derived from the erosion of the Appalachian Mountains. Graphic by Trista L. Thornberry-Ehrlich (Colorado State University), using online information from the North Carolina Geological Survey (http://www.geology.enr.state.nc.us/).

Geologic Issues

The Geologic Resources Division held a Geologic Resources Inventory scoping session for Carl Sandburg Home National Historic Site on May 10–12, 2000, to discuss geologic resources, address the status of geologic mapping, and assess resource management issues and needs. A follow-up conference call was held on May 3, 2011 to update information from the original meeting. This section synthesizes these scoping discussions, in particular those issues that may require attention from resource managers. Contact the Geologic Resources Division for technical assistance.

Landscape Preservation

As described in the park's 2003 General Management Plan, the historic landscape of the park is managed as a cultural resource. This includes preserving viewsheds, restoring historic structures, and maintaining the landscape around them. This goal requires assessing and in some cases mitigating the continuous natural processes of erosion and weathering. Maintaining this landscape often means resisting natural geologic changes, which presents several management challenges. For example, park staff are removing vegetation (usually exotic species) as part of normal maintenance (Woolsey and Walker 2008). Removal of vegetation may expose underlying soils to erosion.

The domes of granitic gneiss underlying the park are exposed as bedrock outcrops throughout the park (fig. 3). These feature prominently in the history of the estate and they exerted substantial influence on Carl Sandburg. As described in the "Geologic Features and Processes" section, these bedrock exposures host unique vegetation communities and contribute to various components of the ecosystem, including xeric (dry) soils, groundwater seeps, lichen and moss communities, vascular plant communities, and landscape patterns (table 1). During Sandburg's tenure at the site, many of the outcrops were left overgrown, due to the family's relaxed management style, and as a matter of practicality (Jones 2005). Today, the domes are also subjects of regular maintenance, including the manual removal of encroaching saplings and mechanical, chemical, and manual removal of invasive species (Woolsey and Walker 2008).

In 2011, more than 89,700 people visited the park, with most visitation during the summer months. With increasing local population, visitation is expected to continue to rise. These visitors are placing increasing demands on the resources of the park. Over 8 km (5 mi) of trails at Carl Sandburg Home lead visitors through mountain and forest ecosystems. The vegetation communities of the gneiss outcrops within the park are particularly vulnerable to degradation from foot traffic; the particular flora within these communities is slow to recover from disturbance (Woolsey and Walker 2008). In addition to the potential for visitors slipping and falling on the bare exposures of bedrock in the park, foot traffic could dislodge rocks and pebbles, sending them tumbling to lower slopes, trails, and other visitor use

facilities (M. Carter, geologist, U.S. Geological Survey, I. Van Hoff, biological science technician, and J. DeYoung, chief of resources and facility management, Carl Sandburg Home NHS, conference call, May 3, 2011). Little Glassy Mountain has very steep rock faces. Visitors have developed a social trail to bedrock exposures around the summit of Little Glassy Mountain, which leads over exposed rocks to reach a boardwalk below. This trail has high potential for visitor injury: sliding on slippery spots; falling on wet, woody debris; and dislodging rocks and pebbles down to the boardwalk below (I. Van Hoff and J. DeYoung, conference call, May 3, 2011). Trails and park roads are eroding. At least 15 cm (6 in.) of soil and trail base has eroded from the Five Points trail intersection area since the marker was installed in 1973 (I. Van Hoff and J. DeYoung, conference call, May 3, 2011) (fig. 4).

Trail runoff threatens the unique bedrock outcrop plant communities by artificially introducing sedimentation that disturbs lichen and moss communities; this also has the potential to accelerate the process of flora succession on outcrops. This issue is apparent along the Big Glassy Trail and on the slopes of Little Glassy Mountain (fig. 5) (Woolsey and Walker 2008). Woolsey and Walker (2008) describe various management strategies for preserving these ecosystems and balancing visitor access and historic preservation. The preferred strategy involves restricting access to sites of high conservation values through regulations or interpretive materials. Under this strategy, rock outcrops within the park are categorized as 1) 'discovery sites,' i.e., outcrops accessible by visitors on park trails to appreciate the viewshed; 2) 'cultural sites' which are outcrops located near buildings or structures that are part of the park's historical landscape; and 3) 'conservation sites,' which are outcrops that support significant biodiversity and are located away from the park's designated trail system (Woolsey and Walker 2008). This strategy would maintain visitor access, but diminish the use of social trails, with the goal of reducing the impacts of erosion and sedimentation on the park's landscape.

Water-related Issues

In the moist climate of the central-southern Appalachian Mountains, abundant runoff water flows in streams, rivers, springs, and into ponds, eventually percolating down into the fracture system aquifer of the Henderson

Augen Gneiss (geologic map unit Chg) in the Carl Sandburg Home National Historic Site area (Alfano 1993). There are a variety of resource management issues associated with water quality; stream flow, channel morphology, and sediment loading; ponds, lakes, and springs; and wetlands. Those with geologic components are mentioned here. Contact the NPS Water Resources Division (http://nature.nps.gov/water/) for guidance and technical assistance regarding water issues.

Water Quality

There are a variety of anthropogenic impacts to local water quality, but the park's underlying geology also contributes to water quality issues. Naturally, rainwater is mildly acidic, a condition exacerbated by air pollution. This acidity can be offset by the neutralizing potential of soluble rocks such as limestone, a source of bicarbonate ions. Unlike limestones, the granitic-composition metamorphic gneiss that underlies the park is relatively insoluble, and does not have much capacity to buffer acidic meteoric water. Therefore springs within the park have pH that falls below the state standard for freshwater, which is a pH between 6 and 9 (Meiman 2005; I. Van Hoff and J. DeYoung, conference call, May 3, 2011). Acidic meteoric water contributes to acidic soils that support specific habitats, including acidic cove forests of the southern Appalachians.

As part of the water quality inventory and monitoring effort for the NPS Cumberland Piedmont Network, four sampling sites exist within Carl Sandburg Home National Historic Site: Trout Pond Spring, Side Lake, Mountain Reservoir, and Front Lake (Meiman 2005). Measurements are collected four times per year, every other year (Meiman 2007, 2008). Parameters measured include: temperature, specific conductance, pH, dissolved oxygen, acid-neutralizing capacity, fecal coliform bacteria, discharge, anions-cations, total organic carbon, total suspended solids, chlorophyll, atrazine, and turbidity (Meiman 2005). Although they are naturally acidic, waters at the park are consistently the highest quality with respect to the measured parameters within the network (Meiman 2008).

Stream Flow, Channel Morphology, and Sediment Load

There are three streams within the park (Meiman 2005; I. Van Hoff, written communication, March 19, 2012). The first is Memminger Creek, which has an east and a west branch. The west branch originates in the park above Mountain Reservoir. The east branch originates on private land southeast of the park. The branches join outside park boundaries, at the confluence becoming Memminger Creek proper. The creek then flows into Ravenswood Lake (outside of park), draining from Ravenswood Lake, the creek immediately re-enters park at the Front Lake and finally exits the park as Memminger Creek under Little River Road. The second is the creek originating at Wellington's Spring at the foot of Little Glassy Mountain. This creek ("Wellington's Creek") flows into Trout Pond and then Side Lake. The third is an unnamed tributary originating on Glassy Mountain west of the park boundary. It joins "Wellington's Creek" at the west end of Side Pasture

within the park, crosses the pastures and flows into Side Lake. Flow from Side Lake joins Memminger Creek just inside the park boundary, exiting under Little River Road. The U.S. Geological Survey WaterWatch program maintains a website of streamgage data in the Henderson County area: http://waterwatch.usgs.gov/new/index.php?sno=Henderson%2C+NC&ds=dv01d_por&btnGo=GO&m=sitempnn.

Channel morphology changes, especially during flooding, affect nearby cultural as well as geological resources by threatening the stability of stream banks, creating potential for collapse. Intense precipitation events may also result in periodic deposits of deep sediments. Sediment load is an indicator of the level of erosion upstream. Sediment loading can result in changes to channel morphology and overbank flooding frequency. This in turn can impact riparian zones flanking streams. Much of the land within the watershed of the park streams is either already developed or steep wilderness. With limited potential for additional development, there is limited concern for an associated increase in sediment load (I. Van Hoff, written communication, March 19, 2012).

Lord et al. (2009) provide an overview of river and stream dynamics, describe potential triggers of channel instability, and describe methods to monitor streams and rivers. Stream channel morphology is influenced by complex interrelationships between regional geology, climate, topographic gradient, drainage basin history, river history, and sediment load. Channel instability manifests via significant changes in channel bed elevation, cross-sectional morphology, and channel pattern changes. Vital signs, a subset of characteristics of a fluvial system that can be monitored to provide information about the condition and trends of a system, include: 1) watershed landscape (vegetation, land use, surficial geology, slopes, and hydrology), 2) hydrology (frequency, magnitude, and duration of stream flow rates), 3) sediment transport (rates, modes, sources, and types of sediment), 4) channel cross-section, 5) channel planform (outline as viewed from above), and 6) channel longitudinal profile (Lord et al. 2009).

Ponds, Lakes, and Springs

There are five lakes and ponds within the park: Front Lake, Duck Pond, Mountain Reservoir, Trout Pond, and Side Lake. They are all rather small (the smallest are less than one-tenth of an acre), anthropogenic, and impounded by dams. They predate the Sandburg residency and were largely neglected until the NPS acquired the property (I. Van Hoff and J. DeYoung, conference call, May 3, 2011). The ponds and lakes are managed by the NPS as historic features, and will be preserved as part of the historic landscape. The primary issues associated with the park's lakes and ponds include debris collection, sedimentation (fig. 6) and dredging, and dam maintenance. Front Lake and Side Lake were dredged in the 1980s. Masonry of the Trout Pond dam could be repointed and minor seepage occurs at the Front Lake and Side Lake dams. Three check dams along streams within the park have completely filled with sediment and are no longer functional (I. Van Hoff, written communication, March 19, 2012).

Several natural springs occur within the park, flowing through and emerging from fractures in the Henderson Augen Gneiss bedrock. Near the goat barn, two small springs join to form a small stream used by the Sandburg's to water the animals. This stream also supplied the main house, prior to its connection to municipal water supplies (I. Van Hoff and J. DeYoung, conference call, May 3, 2011). Approximately 90 m (300 ft) upslope from Mountain Reservoir, a small spring emerges from the bedrock, flows through the reservoir and continues downhill, flowing over rock outcrops in a bedrock channel. No official park trails lead to this site, but its aesthetic appeal probably attracts visitors to this remote area of the park (I. Van Hoff and J. DeYoung, conference call, May 3, 2011). The Mountain Reservoir site represents the headwaters of the Front Lake watershed (Meiman 2005). Trout Pond Spring emerges approximately 100 m (300 ft) upstream of impounded Trout Pond. It is a small perennial spring and is the headwater of the Side Lake watershed. Prior to 2003, the NPS buried the spring under rubble and installed a spring-box and supply tank for the barn operation (Meiman 2005).

Wetlands

Wetlands, areas where the water table is at or near the ground surface for at least part of the year, are significant ecological communities in the Appalachian Mountains. Some wetlands, such as ephemeral ponds, dry out seasonally, allowing a fish-free environment needed by several amphibian species for breeding. A large number of rare, threatened and endangered species thrive in these wetlands. In addition to providing habitat for numerous rare species, wetlands serve a number of important ecological functions. During major storm events, wetlands absorb some of the excess storm water and slowly release the extra water into downstream areas. This greatly reduces flooding and maintains groundwater levels.

Historically, human activities have impacted or destroyed wetlands. Many early federal programs (e.g. the Swamplands Act of 1850) provided incentives to landowners for "improving" wetlands. As a result, many wetlands were ditched, drained and filled in. These efforts resulted in a substantial loss of wetlands throughout North America.

The park preserves valuable, diverse wetland habitat. It took more than 120 years for most of the provisions of the Swamplands Act of 1850 to be reversed by the Wetland Protection Act of 1972. In North Carolina at least 49% of all wetland acreage was lost between the 1780s and 1980s (Mitsch and Gosselink 1993). This loss has resulted in the decline of many native species of wetland-dependent waterfowl and wildlife. Urban development today continues to drain and fill wetlands.

Carl Sandburg Home National Historic Site contains some of the few remaining pristine, high-elevation wetlands in North Carolina. These include an herbaceous vegetation meadow, a white water lily aquatic wetland, and a rush marsh.

Seismicity

Carl Sandburg Home National Historic Site occasionally experiences minor earthquakes. The largest earthquake (magnitude 5.2) in western North Carolina occurred just west of Asheville on February 21, 1916. This event destroyed chimneys, cracked windows, and sent residents running into the streets (Stover and Coffman 1993). In the spring of 2011, earthquakes were locally heard, but not felt. Seismicity in western North Carolina is likely caused by tectonic stresses associated with the rising Appalachian Mountains. As the mountains are worn away by erosion, they rise like a boat whose load has been removed (isostasy). Preexisting zones of weakness (faults) are reactivated to accommodate stress, resulting in earthquakes (Beutel et al. 2008).

According to the digital geologic map data for the park, an unnamed thrust fault occurs just 400 m (1,300 ft) east of the park boundary. This ancient fault separates the Henderson Augen Gneiss from the Garnetiferous muscovite schist, amphibolite and hornblende gneiss (geologic map units Chg and CZgms, respectively). Although not very seismically active today, ancient faults and shear zones attest to the intense deformation and rock movement associated with Appalachian Mountain building hundreds of millions of years ago. Flat Rock, North Carolina is within the Brevard fault zone. Ancient fault zones, such as the Brevard zone, are no longer active and are considered "aseismic" (M. Carter, geologist, U.S. Geological Survey, professional communication, May 3, 2011). According to the U.S. Geological Survey's national seismic hazard map of 2008, Carl Sandburg Home National Historic Site is located between two areas of moderate to moderately-high hazard, one of which trends along the eastern margin of Tennessee south into Georgia (moderate), the other centered in Charleston, South Carolina (moderately-high) (Peterson et al. 2008a, 2008b).

Seismic activity is uncommon in the park area. However, even a moderate seismic event could trigger mass wasting on the steep slopes surrounding the park. A 1998 seismic hazard study of six of the buildings at Carl Sandburg Home National Historic Site suggested that the buildings would fare well during a large earthquake. The greatest threat to safety is from failure of the brick chimneys of the Main House (Denver Service Center 1998). Seismic monitoring stations in the area are sparse. Geologists suggested having a seismometer installed at Great Smoky Mountains National Park, to the northwest of Carl Sandburg Home (Connors 2000).

The North Carolina Geological survey has an informational publication addressing seismicity within the state at the following website: http://nc-maps.stores.yahoo.net/earthquakes.html. The U.S.

Geological Survey maintains an earthquake monitoring website: http://earthquake.usgs.gov/eqcenter/recenteqsus/, an earthquake hazards site: http://earthquake.usgs.gov/hazards/, and a North Carolina-specific earthquake website: http://earthquake.usgs.gov/earthquakes/states/?region=North%20Carolina. EarthScope provides real time seismic data recorded from their array of instrumentation, which is being installed systematically across the country (http://www.earthscope.org/).

Seismic monitoring data can be used for many purposes, such as determining the frequency of earthquake activity, evaluating earthquake risk, interpreting the geologic and tectonic activity of an area, and providing an effective vehicle for public information and education (Braile 2009). In the chapter about seismic monitoring in *Geological Monitoring*, published by the Geological Society of America, Braile (2009) highlights methods for seismic monitoring, such as monitoring earthquake activity, analysis and statistics of earthquake activity, analysis of historical and prehistoric earthquake activity, earthquake risk estimation, and geomorphic and geologic indications of active tectonics. Their publication provides guidance for using these vital signs and monitoring methodology.

Mass Wasting

"Mass wasting" refers to any downslope movement of rock, weathered rock material (regolith), or soil. Steep slopes are generally more likely to experience mass wasting. A lack of stabilizing vegetation also increases susceptibility. The lack of vegetation may be natural, such as bedrock balds or other exposures, or exacerbated by human activity, such as social trail creation and subsequent erosion. Mass wasting is not considered a major issue within the park and is not known to occur (J. Van Hoff, written communication, March 19, 2012). It is mentioned here because the combination of steep slopes, exposed bedrock, and climate found in the park are all potential contributors to mass wasting. Small-scale slumps may be developing near Duck Pond or other water features in the park. Wieczorek and Morgan (2008) discussed debris-flow hazards throughout the Appalachian Mountains.

In the chapter about mass wasting monitoring in *Geological Monitoring*, published by the Geological Society of America, Wieczorek and Snyder (2009) described the various types of slope movements and mass wasting triggers, and suggested five methods and "vital signs" for monitoring slope movements: types of landslides, landslide triggers and causes, geologic materials in landslides, measurement of landslide movement, and assessing landslide hazards and risks. Their publication provides guidance for using these vital signs and monitoring methodology.

Figure 3. View from a bedrock bald at Carl Sandburg Home National Historic Site. Bedrock is banded Henderson Augen Gneiss (geologic map unit Chg). Banding forms from the alignment of light and dark colored minerals, a result of the intense heat and pressure that metamorphoses a rock. The Henderson Augen Gneiss metamorphosed during compressional events that culminated in the formation of the Appalachian Mountains. NPS photograph by Tim Connors (NPS Geologic Resources Division).

Table 1. Potentially critical components and processes in granitic dome communities: their associated roles and major threats.

Component	Key Roles	Associated threats
Xeric Soils	Severe conditions support xeric (very dry) plant species that contribute to site diversity.	Disturbance, erosion and sedimentation from trails; compaction from visitors.
Seeps	Seeps support mesophytic (preferring neither wet nor dry) and wetland species, moss, and lichen communities.	Disturbance, erosion and sedimentation from trails; vegetative (mats) spalling.
Lichen and Moss Communities	Affect seedlings, water, and nutrient relations. Relic communities reported on many outcrop systems	Trampling from visitors, atmospheric contaminant deposition.
Vascular Plant Community	Unique suite of habitat-specific and regionally-uncommon species. Contributes substantially to regional biodiversity.	Trampling from visitors, exotic invasions, disturbance to soil substrates, over-collection.
Disturbance	Maintains granitic domes as open. Controls vegetation structure. Determines spatial heterogeneity and species abundances.	Frequency. Response lag and legacy effects from human modifications, particularly disruption of the fire regime.
Landscape pattern	Affects meta-population* dynamics, gene flow	Increasing regional development and associated impacts. Greater insularity of outcrop communities.

Table adapted from Woolsey and Walker (2008). * = A meta-population consists of a group of spatially separated populations of the same species which interact at some level or, in other words, several distinct populations together with areas of suitable habitat which are currently unoccupied.

Figure 4. Erosion is removing material from park trails. This trail marker was installed at ground level in 1973. Since then, at least 15 cm (6 in.) of trail base has eroded away. Park vehicle for scale. NPS photograph courtesy Irene Van Hoff (Carl Sandburg Home NHS).

Figure 5. Sediment deposition. Sediment from runoff along the Glassy Trail is deposited on a bald of Henderson Augen Gneiss. Photograph from Woolsey and Walker (2008).

Figure 6. Duck Pond sediment. Sediment from runoff along the road adjacent to Duck Pond is deposited in and along the banks of the pond. Note erosion and possible slumping across the pond. National Park Service photograph courtesy Irene Van Hoff (Carl Sandburg Home NHS).

Geologic Features and Processes

This section describes the most prominent and distinctive geologic features and processes in Carl Sandburg Home National Historic Site.

Balds

Domes of Henderson Augen Gneiss (geologic map unit Chg) are present throughout the park as bedrock outcrops or "balds." These smooth, light-colored exposures glint when wet in the sunlight, lending to the various "glassy" names in the park area (e.g. Looking Glass, Glassy Bare, Shining Rock, Big Glassy Mountain, and Little Glassy Mountain). As vegetation communities in the southern Appalachians, balds or granitic domes are defined as relatively open areas devoid of trees, occurring as either shrub-dominated areas or grasslands, at or near the summits of the highest mountains at the edges of spruce-fir forests more commonly associated with northern climates in Canada. They are one of the most unusual environments in the mountains of North Carolina and are globally-rare vegetation community types (Woolsey and Walker 2008).

Balds are enigmatic because they occur well below the treeline elevation at North Carolina's latitude, meaning that they would otherwise be expected to be vegetated. They are more common in the higher mountains than in the Inner Piedmont where Carl Sandburg Home National Historic Site is located (Department of Environment and Natural Resources 2010). It is unknown how they formed, or why they still persist as islands amidst the surrounding forest. Theories as to how they formed include that they were ancient fire burns, remnants from cooler ice age climates, or the result of purposeful clearing by American Indians. However, none of these theories adequately explains the persistence of balds. Natural processes of fire, drought, windthrow, and spalling of vegetative mats likely contribute to keeping the balds open (Houle 1990; Woolsey and Walker 2008).

Granitic dome communities are distinguished by differences in vegetation and elevation—the boundary between high- and low-elevation granitic dome communities occurs around 915 m (3,000 ft) above sea level. With elevations in the park reaching a maximum of 823 m (2,700 ft), all the balds within Carl Sandburg Home National Historic Site are low-elevation granitic dome communities. West of the park, high-elevation granitic domes tend to occur in cool, humid areas and have patchy low nutrient, acidic soils (as a result of the abundant precipitation, alkaline components of the soils are washed away) with thick accumulations of organic humus material. They occur commonly at elevations between 1,220 and 1,500 m (4,000 and 4,920 ft). Annual precipitation at these higher elevations frequently exceeds 200 cm (79 in.) per year and average annual temperatures hover near 8 °C (46 °F)—higher precipitation and lower temperatures than at the low-elevation granitic dome community type such as occurs at the park (Shafer 1986; Schafale and Weakley 1990).

Like high-elevation granitic dome communities, low-elevation granitic dome communities occur in exposed positions on peaks, ridgetops, and upper slopes as exfoliated outcrops of granitic rock. Exfoliation is a type of weathering whereby sheets of rocks are removed in layers, exposing rounded fresh surfaces. In contrast to high-elevation granitic dome communities, low-elevation granitic dome communities have more fractured rock, which may allow the growth of deep-rooted woody plants and more soil accumulation (Department of Environment and Natural Resources 2010). An example of a high-elevation granitic dome feature is Flat Laurel Gap. This heath bald and Appalachian bog is located near the park, on the western side of the Pisgah Ridge in the Balsam Mountains.

There are at least nine significant exposures of bald rock occurring in the park, and a comprehensive 2008 vegetation survey revealed the presence of more than 21 different granitic dome bedrock outcrops within the park boundaries (fig. 7) (I. Van Hoff, biological science technician, and J. DeYoung, chief of resources and facility management, Carl Sandburg Home NHS, conference call, May 3, 2011).

Low-elevation granitic dome communities within the park boundaries contribute substantially to biodiversity in the region, harboring unique flora (196 native vascular plant taxa, 33 lichen species, and 16 moss species within park boundaries). According to Woolsey and Walker (2008), these domes are unique in that they form an abrupt, azonal community-type, referring to plant communities which appear in the same form in several different climatic zones because they are determined by the same extreme conditions (soils). Conditions on these domes are arid, very locally xeric (dry) with low fertility. The shallow, poorly-developed soils, extreme temperatures, and drought associated with domes are all environmental stressors for vegetation (Ware and Pinion 1990; Wiser et al. 1996; Woolsey and Walker 2008).

The distribution of this type of community depends strongly on the type and relative resistance of the underlying bedrock. Each outcrop, with its individual elevation and solar radiation characteristics, may host a different vegetational assemblage (Wiser et al. 1996). Unlike other bedrock outcrop community types, bedrock domes of granitic composition tend to be massive, exfoliating rocks with few crevices or irregularities containing soil pockets (Woolsey and Walker 2008). The Henderson Augen Gneiss is resistant to erosion relative to other schistose bedrock in the surrounding areas, and its homogeneity contributes to bald formation. Domes are unlikely to develop in schist

(M. Carter, geologist, U.S. Geological Survey, written communication, September 28, 2011).

Henderson Augen Gneiss

The town of Flat Rock, North Carolina takes its name from a bald underlain by Henderson Augen Gneiss (geologic map unit Chg), regionally referred to as the Henderson gneiss. Generally, gneiss is a foliated (planar minerals are oriented in a similar direction) metamorphic rock that has a banded appearance due to alternating layers of minerals. The word 'augen' is German for "eyes," and refers to the eye-like shape of mineral crystals within the gneiss. The eye-like shape results from compression and stretching that elongates mineral crystals. Augen within the gneiss are important strain markers for this part of the western Inner Piedmont (Bream et al. 1998).

The Henderson gneiss is one of the most extensive lithologic units of the Inner Piedmont of North Carolina, stretching over 5,000 sq km (1,900 sq mi) (Odom and Fullagar 1973; Bream et al. 1998). The Henderson Gneiss is named for exposures in Henderson County, North Carolina (Keith 1905). It is Cambrian in age, approximately 509-535 million years old. Lens-shaped outliers of the main gneiss body extend northeastward in North Carolina in the western Inner Piedmont (Harper et al. 1977; Goldstein and Brown 1985; Vauchez and Brunel 1988; Bream et al. 1998; Giorgis and Hatcher 1999).

Domes of Henderson gneiss are common throughout the area. Initially, granitic magma plumes intruded the local country rock (another type of metamorphic rock called mica schist). The schistose rocks are less resistant to weathering than the granitic gneiss. Over time, the schist weathers away leaving domes of more-resistant granitic gneiss behind (M. Carter, conference call, May 3, 2011).

Although the composition of the Henderson gneiss is generally closer to granite, it is sometimes subdivided into an augen gneiss (as in the park) and a biotite granitic gneiss (Lemmon 1981). The augen gneiss ranges in composition from quartz monzonite to granodiorite, with large crystals of potassium-rich, alkali feldspar (microcline) up to 2.5 cm (1 in.) in diameter. Parallel-aligned, dark, platy biotite crystals define the characteristic banded pattern in the rocks known as foliation (fig. 8). Locally, the gneiss is highly deformed, with many pervasive brittle zones, another indicator of its origin in a zone of continental collision. The augen gneiss was metamorphosed under relatively high temperature and pressure conditions (upper amphibolite facies) (Lemmon 1981; Yanagihara and Davis 1992).

The Henderson gneiss is featured in many theses and dissertations produced at the University of Tennessee, Knoxville including Liu (1991), Davis (1993), Giorgis (1999), and Hill (1999). These types of manuscripts provide local and regional geologic overviews that may aid the resource managers at Carl Sandburg Home National Historic Site to understand the geologic setting and history of the area.

Geology and History Connections

A primary goal of the Carl Sandburg Home National Historic Site is to maintain the historical context of the area. The Carl Sandburg home is an example of a country house, and it also contains aspects significant to Appalachian Mountain history. This history extends beyond European settlement, to the early fields, trading routes, and settlements of the American Indians. The Cherokee Indians of North Carolina, and the Monacan, Saponi, and Tutelo Indians of western Virginia, were among the earliest inhabitants of the Blue Ridge area.

Bedrock balds such as those within and surrounding the park are thought to have been points of rendezvous for trade and ceremonial significance (McDaniel 2000). The domes of Henderson Augen Gneiss in the area were important hunting grounds for the Cherokee (Johnson 2003), likely due to their inherent high visibility in contrast with the dense forests and the concentration of forest-edge habitat (Woolsey and Walker 2008). Native people left artifacts and geomorphological changes in the landscape, such as fields at the base of the mountains, artifacts of the American Indian agricultural method of burning and clearing the trees and underbrush to create crop and hunting land.

After the Treaty of Hopewell with the Cherokees in 1785, Europeans began settling the area, clearing land, and introducing livestock grazing (Jones 2005). A road passed through Flat Rock by the 1830s (Jones 2005). By the mid-1800s and early 1900s, the Blue Ridge was viewed as a desirable location for persons of wealth to build country retreats. One notable example is the Biltmore Estate, outside of Asheville, North Carolina. Flat Rock is centered in a famous pre-Civil War resort community in western North Carolina. Here, wealthy citizens from cities like Charleston, South Carolina sought refuge from heat and common city diseases during the summer months.

Carl Sandburg Home National Historic Site typifies this desire for a country escape; however, it was also always a working farm estate. The landscape surrounding the home is rural with trails and ponds (figs. 1 and 9). The local geology figured prominently in the early history of the working farm. It was originally called 'Rock Hill,' by the estate's founder, Christopher G. Memminger (the first Secretary of the Treasury of the Confederate States of America), because of its "barren" landscape (Jones 2005). It was renamed 'Connemara,' after the rocky, pastoral landscape of western Ireland (Jones 2005). Both of these names were inspired by prominent bedrock outcrops of Henderson Augen Gneiss present within the park.

The Sandburg's inherited many of the historic farmstead features when they purchased the property in 1945, including the impounded lakes and ponds. Previous owner Ellison Smyth was responsible for the addition of Side Lake, and for constructing a trail to the open bald at the summit of Big Glassy Mountain (Jones 2005). Construction on the main house started in the 1830s on the steep slopes of Glassy Mountain. To provide the building site on the steep slope, a series of three level terraces were constructed, each running east and west across the hillside (Jones 2005).

At the time, most plantation homes sourced material from nearby quarries and forests (M. Carter, conference call, May 3, 2011). When Memminger owned the property, he used oxen and mules to haul stone from a nearby quarry. Clay bricks for chimneys and lumber were acquired locally (Jones 2005). This was prior to the widespread use of dynamite for rock extraction, and the only "workable" quarry was on the nearby Tranquility estate (Jones 2005). The main house and outbuildings have stone foundations. The stone-walled ground floor raised the first floor 3 m (8 to 9 ft) above grade at the front of the house (Jones 2005). There are many rock walls, stone culverts, and dams, similarly sourced from local rocks. Some of the dams, including that of the lake at the foot of the hill from the Main House, date back to Memminger's tenure during the 1850s (Jones 2005). These "non-natural outcrops" could provide interpretive tangibles for visitor programs.

Natural themes are featured throughout Carl Sandburg's works; clearly, the landscape of his home influenced his life and work. During Sandburg's 22-year tenure at Connemara (1945–1967), he published more than one-third of his literary works. The large rock outcrop behind the Main House was a favorite writing spot. Carl Sandburg often worked outdoors and left a cane chair on the outcrop to sit and write in the sun (see inside cover) (Steichen 1982). This same outcrop served as a family picnic site, whereas an outcrop near Side Lake was used for sunning and picnics (Woolsey and Walker 2008). Sandburg often reflected on his outdoor inspiration, including in these words to a friend:

> "It is necessary now and then for a man to go away by himself and experience loneliness; to sit on a rock in the forest and to ask of himself, 'Who am I, and where have I been, and where am I going?'...If one is not careful, one allows diversions to take up one's time-the stuff of life."
>
> —Carl Sandburg,
> from a letter to friend Ralph McGill

The author and his family "would walk a 'measured mile' returning by starlight, often with a souvenir of acorns, rocks or leaves" (National Park Service 2011). Sandburg's rock collection included three or four fossils now part of the park's museum collections: marine invertebrates and leaf impressions in limestone, crinoids in conglomerates, crinoids in sandstone, and a brachiopod (Hunt-Foster et al. 2009; I. Van Hoff and J. DeYoung, conference call, May 3, 2011). Fossils are not found in gneiss nor other high-grade metamorphic rocks. They would have been destroyed by the intense heat and pressure associated with continental collisions and mountain building. Thus, the fossils were not collected within the park or surrounding area, but are likely from areas on the western side of the Blue Ridge Mountains. The closest fossiliferous rocks are near

Knoxville, Tennessee (M. Carter, conference call, May 3, 2011). This collection is an example of how paleontological and geological resources can be interpretive tangibles with regards to the cultural resource contexts in which they occur (Kenworthy and Santucci 2006).

Geology and Biodiversity

Numerous factors determine the types of flora and fauna a particular area can support, including the geologic framework (bedrock, structures, regolith, topography, etc.), the extent of geomorphic processes, climate, orientation (north- versus south-facing slopes), elevation, and soil characteristics. The geologic framework influences the mineral content and thickness of the soil, as well as overall drainage, which in turn determines the species that can grow there. Topography affects what grows where: south-facing slopes tend to be warmer and drier, because the day-long presence of the sun evaporates soil moisture. On the other hand, north-facing slopes are more shaded and therefore cooler and moister, but they generally take the brunt of the coldest and strongest winds that impact the size and type of vegetation.

For a small park, Carl Sandburg Home National Historic Site contains incredible biodiversity. As part of the Southern Appalachians, the park is located in one of the most diverse deciduous forest ecosystems in the world (Pittillo et al. 1980). At Carl Sandburg Home National Historic Site, an inventory by the National Park Service in 2001 identified 14 distinct plant communities and more than 135 newly documented vascular plant species species on the 108-ha (262-ac) property (White 2003). These are included in the 540 documented vascular plant species at the park from the on-site herbarium (The Nature Conservancy and the National Park Service 1996-1997). A retired scientist collected 281 specimens of mosses, lichens, and liverworts at the park between 1996 and 1998, further demonstrating the ecological importance of the area (fig. 10). Diversity of habitats and living species are a hallmark of Carl Sandburg Home. Indeed, diversity is a key concept in an understanding of the ecology of the Appalachian Mountains. For thousands of years, certain areas of the southern Appalachians provided a refugium for species displaced by glacial ice advances far to the north during the Pleistocene, and habitat for colder climate species that thrived when the ice retreated.

The flora at Carl Sandburg Home are associated with a pine woodland, a dry chestnut-oak forest, an acidic Appalachian cove forest (growing on acidic soils formed by leaching of alkaline components and lack of pH buffering potential of the Henderson Augen Gneiss bedrock) and montane oak-hickory forest, a semi-natural wooded upland, an herbaceous vegetation meadow, a white water lily aquatic wetland, a rush marsh, and a "flat rock community". As described above, the flat rock refers to the Appalachian low-elevation granitic dome of Henderson gneiss upon which beak rush and broom sedge grow in thin soil. This last association is ranked "G2," or 'globally very rare' among geologic outcrop communities. These findings illustrate that even relatively small parks can be sites of tremendous biodiversity.

Small parks like Carl Sandburg Home National Historic Site are becoming refuges for native plants threatened by exotic species and development. The park lies in one of the most rapidly growing counties in North Carolina. Inventories provide the scientific information needed to preserve the unique natural heritage of this small mountain park. Understanding the relationships and connectivity between geology and the ecosystem founded upon it contributes to preservation of native ecosystems at the park.

The eastern edge of the mountain ranges is consistently more rugged and steep than the western edge, due to the direction of uplift during the creation of the Appalachian Mountains. Connections between geological features and resources and biological resources could be highlighted during biological inventory and monitoring efforts, to facilitate resource management and, perhaps, even predict occurrences or distribution.

Forests of the Balsam Mountains

Multiple and overlapping ecosystems, exceptional examples of forest communities, and locally wide variations yield high diversity in the Balsam Mountains. The Balsam Mountains have at least seven forest types (oak-chestnut forests, cove hardwood forests, floodplain forests, oak-pine forests, northern hardwood forests, orchards, and spruce-fir forests), primarily due to their elevation range, from bogs at lower elevations to spruce-fir on Balsam Knob, which reaches 1,954 m (6,410 ft)

(McDaniel 2000). As mentioned earlier, factors such as geology, topography, orientation, and climate affect the development of these forests.

According to McDaniel (2000), oak-chestnut forests are perhaps the most common in Western North Carolina. The cove hardwood forest develops in protected coves with damp, mesic soils, generally at low and middle elevations (McDaniel 2000; I. Van Hoff, conference call, May 3, 2011). The conditions here are ideal for an amazing diversity of trees—as many as 40 species in one forest. The floodplain forest, unique in Western North Carolina, and restricted to the Asheville and French Broad River basins, is related to the cove hardwood forest. One of the driest forests, the oak-pine forest, grows in thin and sandy soil that does not produce the lush vegetation usually so prevalent in the mountains. Blueberry bushes (*Vaccinium*), mountain laurel (*Kalmia latifolia*), and a limited number of hardy wildflowers are sufficiently drought resistant to grow here. With its diverse trees and under story, the northern hardwoods forest resembles forests found in New York and New England and features species common to the northern regions. Trees include yellow birch, yellow buckeye, and beech, among others. A variation on the northern hardwood forest, orchards, occurs when northern red oaks dominate areas where harsh weather stunts trees in ways that make them look like fruit orchards. An example of this is at Frying Pan Gap, on the Blue Ridge Parkway just south of Pisgah Inn. Spruce-fir forests are only found at higher elevations and higher latitudes in places such as New England and Canada. Spruce appears at 1,370 m (4,500 ft) elevation while the fir requires another 1,000 m (3,000 ft) elevation before it can grow.

Figure 7. Map of the outcrops of Henderson Augen Gneiss (geologic map unit symbol Chg) or "granitic domes" that occur within Carl Sandburg Home National Historic Site. Graphic adapted from figure 1 in Woolsey and Walker (2008) by Trista L. Thornberry-Ehrlich (Colorado State University).

Figure 8. Banding and foliation formed within the Henderson Augen Gneiss at Carl Sandburg Home National Historic Site. Banding formed during intense heating and pressure associated with mountain building, culminating in the formation of the Appalachian Mountains. Light colored bands contain coarse-grained feldspar crystals, whereas the darker bands contain flaky biotite crystals and other opaque minerals. National Park Service photograph by Tim Connors (NPS Geologic Resources Division).

Figure 9. Historic photograph (ca. 1890) of Connemara, then called Rock Hill due to the prevalence of bedrock exposures, atop a slope above Front Lake and the front pasture (see fig. 1). National Park Service photograph.

Figure 10. Lichen growing on an exposure of Henderson Augen Gneiss at Carl Sandburg Home National Historic Site. National Park Service photograph by Tim Connors (NPS Geologic Resources Division).

Geologic History

This section describes the rocks and unconsolidated deposits that appear on the digital geologic map of Carl Sandburg National Historic Site, the environment in which those units were deposited, and the timing of geologic events that formed the present landscape.

The Henderson Augen Gneiss—the only bedrock geologic map unit mapped within the park—reflects the geologic history of the Inner Piedmont. Rocks of the Inner Piedmont were metamorphosed, uplifted, faulted and folded during several mountain-building events (orogenies), ultimately culminating in the Appalachian Mountains and the assembly of the supercontinent Pangaea. Hundreds of millions of years of subsequent erosion have exposed the core of this mountain range in the Piedmont.

The digital geologic map (GIS) data for Carl Sandburg Home National Historic Site extends beyond the boundaries of the park, and includes additional geologic map units that vary in age and composition. The rocks range from ridgetop Precambrian and Paleozoic gneisses that are hundreds of millions of years old (geologic map units Chg and SOgg), mylonites (CZmy), and other metamorphic rocks (CZts, CZgms, and CZtgn), to unconsolidated, recent (likely no more than 2 million years old) Quaternary-age sediments including stream alluvium (Qal) and other unmapped deposits such as blockfall or colluvium which line valleys and cover mountain slopes.

The rocks in the park represent a long geologic history of deposition, metamorphism and deformation, mountain building, and erosional processes that shaped today's landscape. Figure 11 outlines the general geologic history of the southern Appalachian Mountains, from the Precambrian through the Alleghany Orogeny prior to regional erosion.

Proterozoic Eon (2,500–542 million years ago): Ancient Mountain Building and Iapetus Ocean Formation

More than one billion years ago, the Grenville Orogeny deformed and metamorphosed a large continental mass ancestral to North America, called Laurentia, as part of the assembly of a supercontinent called Rodinia (fig. 12). The regional sedimentation, deformation, intrusion of molten material (plutonism), and volcanism are manifested in the metamorphic gneisses in the core of the modern Blue Ridge Mountains west of the park. Fragments of the billion-year-old supercontinent are visible at Blowing Rock in northern North Carolina and Red Top Mountain in northern Georgia (Clark 2001). All of the central Blue Ridge west of Asheville, North Carolina also contain Grenville basement rocks.

Beginning between about 750 to 700 million years ago, rifting of Rodinia led to the opening of the Iapetus Ocean and formed a new eastern margin of the Laurentian continent. The Iapetus was one of several ocean basins that closed episodically during the Paleozoic. Other basins included the Theic and Rheic oceans (Horton and Zullo 1991; Nance and Linnemann 2008). The Rheic Ocean opened during the Early Ordovician, following rifting along the northern margin of Gondwana (another ancient landmass that contained most of the present Southern Hemisphere continents) in the Middle to Late Cambrian (Nance and Linnemann 2008). It widened at the expense of the Iapetus Ocean as the Carolina terrane (described below) drifted towards Laurentia (Nance and Linnemann 2008).

Locally, the Ocoee basin formed on the margin of the supercontinent in what are now western North Carolina, eastern Tennessee and northern Georgia. This basin collected large amounts of the mud, silt, and sand sediments eroded from the Grenville Orogeny-created highlands. These ocean sediments would later form the rocks of today's Appalachian Mountains (Moore 1988). The basin subsided as sediments were deposited, making room for further sedimentation (Tull and Li 1998). The rocks of the Ocoee group today display vast thicknesses (about 15 km or 9 mi), representative of this depositional setting (Clark 2001). Ocoee Group rocks form the bedrock of the Great Smoky, Unicoi, and Balsam Mountains west of Carl Sandburg Home National Historic Site. As rifting continued, volcanism occurred locally in areas of present day Virginia, North Carolina, Tennessee, and Georgia. This igneous activity is largely responsible for the economic deposits of copper, zinc, iron, and sulfur in the eastern United States. The deposits formed when hot, metal-bearing fluids vented onto the floor of the Ocoee basin (Clark 2001). Such economic deposits were among the first mined in the early 1800s of the then-new United States of America.

Paleozoic Era (542–251 million years ago): Building the Appalachians and Assembling Pangaea

Throughout the Paleozoic, fragments of oceanic crust and basin sediments, volcanic island arcs, and other continental land masses collided with the eastern edge of the North American continent, the larger of which are called terranes. Many of these myriad fragments accreted to Laurentia in several episodes of compression accompanied by metamorphism and magmatism. These compressional events of varying duration and intensity affected different but overlapping segments of the eastern edge of North America (figs. 11 and 13) (Horton and Zullo 1991).

During the early Paleozoic, subduction-related volcanic arcs, slabs of oceanic crust, and basin sediments were amalgamating off the eastern margin of the North American continent. Within the Carolina terrane, high-grade metamorphosed volcanic rocks, which had been deeply buried, were moved upwards along major "shear zones" to be juxtaposed against shallow, low-grade metamorphosed volcanic and metamorphosed sedimentary rocks (Secor et al. 1998). Several phases of deformation occurred within the Carolina terrane before it collided with ancestral North America (Butler and Secor 1991).

Taconic Orogeny

Many of the terranes, now located northwest of the Carolina terrane, were accreted, deformed, and metamorphosed during the Ordovician Taconic Orogeny, from about 470 to 440 million years ago (Horton et al. 1988, 1989a, 1989b; Horton and Zullo 1991). The culmination of the Taconic Orogeny involved a closure of the Iapetus Ocean as a volcanic island arc, once situated within the Iapetus Ocean moved westward and collided with the eastern margin of North America (Nance and Linnemann 2008). Oceanic crust and the volcanic arc were thrust onto the eastern edge of the North American continent along major thrust faults (Moore 1988; Connelly and Woodward 1990).

Neoacadian Orogeny, Henderson Gneiss, and the Brevard Zone

The collision of additional landmasses with North America during the Devonian Period signaled the onset of the Neoacadian Orogeny, as the African continent slowly approached between 410 and 360 million years ago. The Inner Piedmont is considered the metamorphic core of the Neoacadian orogeny in the Southern Appalachians (Hatcher et al. 1994; Hill 1999). It contains a series of thin thrust sheets and many large-scale folds and deformation features (Hatcher 1993). The folded complex of rock within the Inner Piedmont was carried northwestward on a major thrust fault. Smaller thrust sheets were emplaced along smaller faults from the northwest to the southeast.

The Henderson Augen Gneiss in western North Carolina is a dominant geologic map unit of the western Inner Piedmont (Yanagihara and Davis 1992). It is bounded by thrust faults. Internal textures and truncated or folded contacts with adjacent rocks suggest that the gneiss began as a large body of granitic material that was folded during regional metamorphism and deformation associated with mountain building (Bream et al. 1998; Bier et al. 2000). Highly deformed zones (termed "mylonite") within the Henderson gneiss (geologic map units Chg and CZmy) formed during the Neoacadian Orogeny. Younger, granite-like plutons subsequently intruded the main body of gneiss approximately 438 million years ago in North Carolina.

Deciphering the geologic history of the southern Appalachians has been notoriously difficult for geologists. Age-dating techniques can help determine discrete events in a particular rock unit's history,

including their crystallization and metamorphism, but these vary for the Henderson gneiss (Davis 1993). Dating isotopes of the minerals rubidium (Rb) and strontium (Sr) found in Henderson gneiss of the Inner Piedmont of Southwestern North Carolina provides an age of 300 million years for the period of maximum metamorphic conditions. These occurred during the Alleghany Orogeny of the Pennsylvanian Period (Goldberg and Fullagar 1993). Hill (1999) dated peak metamorphic and deformation conditions at an older age—between 378 and 386 million years ago.

According to Ranson et al (1999), granite-like bodies of rock within the Inner Piedmont, including the Henderson Augen Gneiss, may have been part of a widespread magmatic event, involving the intrusion of numerous igneous plutons that incorporated some pre-existing Proterozoic crust into their molten material during the Ordovician. This conclusion is based on uranium (U)-lead (Pb) age dating of the Henderson Augen Gneiss at 445 million years ago in South Carolina. Dating feldspars within the Henderson gneiss yielded a crystallization age of about 509–535 million years. This study surmised that the gneiss was originally part of the plutonic, volcanic, and associated clastic rocks of an early Paleozoic island arc system (Odom and Fullagar 1973; Bream et al. 1998). This island arc lay off the east coast of the North American Continent, and was involved in an island arc-continent collision in the Middle Ordovician, when it was accreted onto the continent.

Migmatites (similar to geologic map unit CZtgn) and gneisses are exposed in many places along the Blue Ridge Parkway which passes 32 km (20 mi) northwest of Carl Sandburg Home National Historic Site. The Henderson gneiss is the local representative of the pervasive deformation associated with movement along the Brevard fault zone, northwest of the park. The Brevard zone is a major fault zone which separates the much older metamorphic rocks of the Blue Ridge from the younger rocks of the Inner Piedmont of the Southern Appalachian Mountains (figs. 13-15). The Brevard zone is very complex, at least 356 million years old. Most geologists agree that it accommodated large northwestward displacement in at least five different pulses and experienced high-grade metamorphism and intense deformation during mountain building events that overlap spatially and temporally (Odom and Fullagar 1973; Liu 1991; Hatcher et al. 1994; Hill 1999; Garner et al. 2001). The Henderson Augen Gneiss becomes progressively more deformed to a mylonite as it gets closer to the Brevard Zone (Goldstein and Brown 1985).

Alleghany Orogeny

The Pennsylvanian-Permian Alleghany Orogeny (about 330–270 million years ago) involved the continental collision between Laurentia and Gondwanaland, forming a supercontinent called Pangaea and finally closing the Rheic Ocean (Horton and Zullo 1991; Nance and Linneman 2008; C. S. Howard, South Carolina Geological Survey, written communication, 2009). The deformation associated with the Alleghany Orogeny overprints many previous structures in the southern Appalachians (Schaeffer 1982; C. S. Howard, written communication, 2009). Pre-existing faults such as the Miller Cove and other Paleozoic faults were reactivated as planes of weakness by the Great Smoky thrust fault. This combined with the extremely large strains and lack of strain markers makes restoration of any pre-Alleghany deformation difficult (Connelly and Woodward 1990; Connelly and Woodward 1992).

In the Carolinas, in the vicinity of the park, effects of the Alleghany collision were varied. Major changes included (1) widespread emplacement of molten material (plutonism), (2) westward transport of native and accreted terranes of the Piedmont as part of a thrust sheet or large block of rock that gets pushed along the thrust fault, (3) high temperature and pressure regional metamorphism and deformation, and (4) strike-slip faulting (along shear zones) that sliced and shifted accreting terranes (Horton et al. 1989a 1989b; Horton and Zullo 1991; Butler and Secor 1991; Nance and Linnemann 2008).

Carolina Terrane Accretion

Accretion of the Carolina terrane to Laurentia is a critical unresolved problem in the study of southern Appalachian tectonics (Hibbard 2000). Paleomagnetic data for Paleozoic igneous rocks show that the Carolina terrane had sutured to the continent by approximately 300 million years ago (Butler and Secor 1991). Other geologists favor a much older Late Ordovician to Silurian time of accretion based on magmatism and an uplift event (Hibbard 2000; Hibbard et al. 2002). A study by Hibbard et al. (2002) summarizes this debate and presents a comprehensive history of the Carolina zone that is beyond the scope of this report.

Mesozoic Era (251–65.5 million years ago): Pangaea Separation, Atlantic Ocean Formation, and Appalachian Mountains Erosion

Regardless of when the Carolina Terrane was emplaced, the continental collisions that brought the terrane to the edge of North America were ending. During the Triassic (from about 230 through 200 million years ago), extensional tectonic forces rifted (pulled apart) Pangaea, leading to the continental masses that persist today along a still-widening Atlantic Ocean (fig. 14). Along the eastern margin of North America, normal faulting opened rift basins that rapidly filled with sediment eroded from the highlands of the—at the time—very high and very rugged Appalachian Mountains. Molten material, now preserved as igneous rocks, intruded into the basins as sub-horizontal sheets, or sills, and near-vertical dikes that extend beyond the basins into adjacent rocks.

Associated with the dikes and sills was hydrothermal activity throughout the Piedmont in the Carolinas (Schaeffer 1982; Horton and Zullo 1991; Nystrom 2003; Howard 2004; Horton 2006). Hot, mineral-saturated fluids moved upward, depositing quartz veins containing small amounts of gold. This was the source of the mining interest in the mid-Appalachians area intermittently from 1867 until 1941 (Reed et al. 1980). The frenzy surrounding the gold deposits in Cherokee territory of northern Georgia and North Carolina prompted the removal of the Cherokee people along the march now known as the Trail of Tears (Clark 2001).

Brittle faults, joints, and highly fractured zones developed across the Inner Piedmont and Carolina terranes, during multiple episodes of mid-Mesozoic brittle deformation that accompanied continental rifting (Garihan et al. 1993).

During the Jurassic, at approximately 200 million years ago, the region underwent a period of slow uplift and erosion. The uplift was in response to isostatic adjustments within the crust that forced the continental crust upwards and exposed it to erosion. Since the breakup of Pangaea and the uplift of the Appalachian Mountains, the North American plate has continued to move toward the west. Cenozoic tectonic activity in the Carolinas is manifested in ways such as uplift, subsidence, and faulting (Prowell and Obermeier 1991). Most of this faulting is concentrated in broad, alternating arches (upwarps) and embayments (downwarps) along the southeastern coast (Horton and Zullo 1991).

Running water transported thick deposits of unconsolidated gravel, sand, and silt from the eroding highlands. These were deposited at the base of the mountains as alluvial fans, and spread eastward to become part of the Atlantic Coastal Plain to the east of Carl Sandburg Home National Historic Site (figs. 2 and 15). With fluctuating relative sea level and tectonism throughout the Cenozoic, sediments were regionally deposited and eroded in alternating events. The amount of material eroded from above the now-exposed metamorphic rocks throughout the Piedmont and Blue Ridge is immense. Many of the rocks exposed at the surface must have been at least 20 km (about 10 mi) below the surface prior to regional uplift and erosion!

Cenozoic Era (the past 65.5 million years): Appalachian Mountain Erosion and Ice Age Glaciation

Throughout the Cenozoic, the primary geologic processes at work in the Southern Appalachians were weathering and erosion. The erosion continues today along regional drainage patterns developed during the early Cenozoic, with the large rivers and tributaries stripping sediments, lowering the mountains, and depositing alluvial terraces and alluvium (geologic map unit Qal) along the rivers and shaping the present landscape (Moore 1988; Nystrom 2003; Howard 2004; Horton 2006). Rain, frost, rooted plants, rivers and streams, chemical dissolution, and mass wasting are wearing away the once-craggy peaks. These processes have reduced the Blue Ridge and Balsam Mountains from Himalaya-like proportions to the low profile of one of the world's oldest mountain ranges. Layers of resistant rocks, such as the Henderson Augen Gneiss (Chg), underlie local ridges and mountains. This more resistant rock unit underlies ecologically significant bedrock bald habitats within the park. Mantling the slopes throughout the area are deposits of talus and colluvium, attesting to continuing erosion and weathering.

From about 2.6 million to 11,000 years ago, the ice ages of the Pleistocene resulted in significant changes to Earth's landscape. Though continental ice sheets never reached the southern Appalachians, the colder climates of the ice ages played a role in the geomorphology of the area. The landforms and deposits visible today were probably shaped during the late Tertiary to Quaternary, when a wetter climate, sparse vegetation, and frozen ground caused increased precipitation and runoff that fed ancestral rivers. These conditions enhanced downcutting and erosion (Schultz and Seal 1997). Many of the concentrations of boulders, block fields, and fine-textured colluvium on the forested mountainsides of the Southern Appalachians record the process of frost wedging.

The unique flora and fauna of Great Smoky Mountains National Park, the Blue Ridge Parkway, and Carl Sandburg Home National Historic Site are a result of ancient species migrating south ahead of the advancing glacial front (Clark 2001). Species such as the saw-whet owl, common to northern climates, are established in the southern Appalachians. Forests in the Balsam Mountains include northern hardwood forests and spruce-fir forests, both of which are prevalent in northern latitudes. The specific elevation, climate, orientation, and geologic framework of the southern Appalachians provide habitats for diverse species.

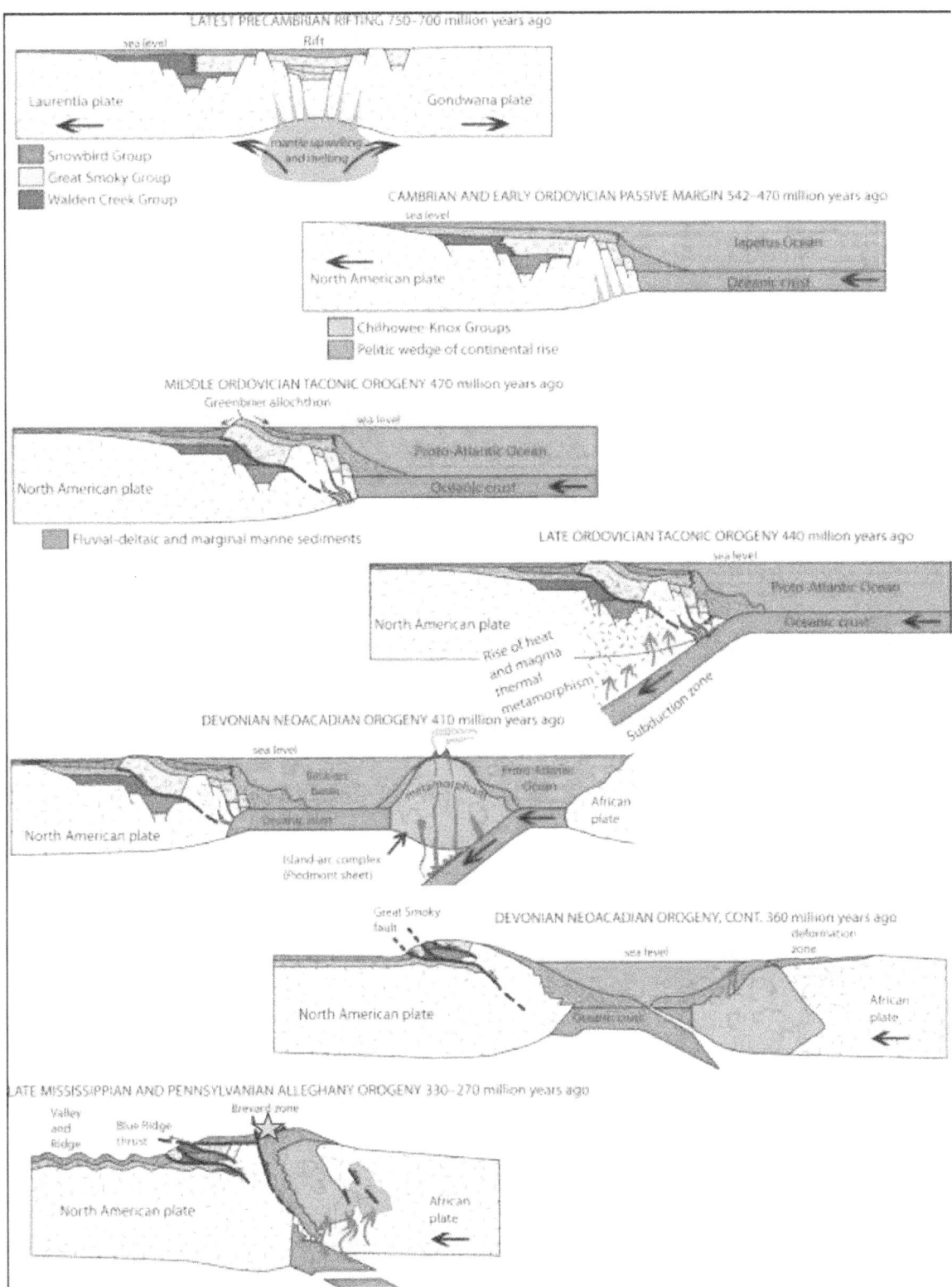

Figure 11. Cross sectional view of the evolution of the Southern Appalachian Mountains from the Precambrian to Pennsylvanian. Following Precambrian rifting and passive margin deposition, the Taconic orogeny created the Greenbrier allochthon (referring to a body of rock that formed elsewhere and was transported to its current position) and fault as well as regional metamorphism. The Neoacadian orogeny involved collision with an island arc which continued into the Alleghany orogeny with the collision of the African continental plate and the development of the Blue Ridge and Valley and Ridge deformation. Green star in bottom graphic indicates the approximate position of Carl Sandburg Home National Historic Site. Adapted from DeWindt (1975) by Trista L. Thornberry-Ehrlich (Colorado State University).

Eon	Era	Period	Epoch	Ma	Geologic Map Units	North Carolina Events
Phanerozoic	Cenozoic	Quaternary	Holocene	0.01	Qal deposited along streams and rivers	Fluvial processes, erosion of Piedmont and Appalachian Mountains, sediment deposition in Coastal Plain
			Pleistocene			
		Tertiary / Neogene	Pliocene	2.6		
			Miocene	5.3		
				23.0		
		Tertiary / Paleogene	Oligocene	33.9		
			Eocene	55.8		Limestone deposited in Coastal Plain, erosion, and weathering continue
			Paleocene			
				65.5		
	Mesozoic	Cretaceous		145.5	No Mesozoic units are present on the park map	Ongoing erosion and weathering in Piedmont and Appalachian Mountains, Cape Fear Arch begins to develop
		Jurassic		199.6		Rift basins form
		Triassic				Breakup of Pangaea begins; brittle faulting and volcanism
				251		
	Paleozoic	Permian				Supercontinent Pangaea intact
				299		Alleghany (Appalachian) Orogeny; thrust faulting in west, deformation in eastern Piedmont
		Pennsylvanian		318.1		
		Mississippian		359.2		Uplift and erosion
		Devonian		416	Deformation and metamorphism of Chg*, CZmy, and CZtgn	Neoacadian Orogeny, pegmatites emplaced, metamorphism of Carolina slate, erosion
		Silurian		443.7	Intrusion of SOgg	Uplift and erosion
		Ordovician		488.3		Taconic Orogeny, faulting, folding, metamorphism of pre-existing rocks
						Sandstone, shale, and limestone deposited in mountain area, deposition of Carolina slate rocks
		Cambrian			Intrusion of Chg plutons	Extensive oceans cover most of proto-North America (Laurentia)
				542		
Proterozoic		Precambrian		1000	CZmy, CZign, CZgms, and CZts are deposited and/or intruded	Supercontinent rifted apart Sedimentary and volcanic rocks deposited in Piedmont and Blue Ridge, metamorphism
Archean				2500		Grenville Orogeny formed supercontinent, olest dated rock in North Carolina is 1,800 million years old
Hadean				~4000		
				4600	Formation of the Earth	Formation of Earth's crust

(Age of Mammals, Age of Dinosaurs, Age of Amphibians, Fishes, Marine Invertebrates are labeled vertically in the Ma column region.)

Figure 12. Geologic timescale. The timescale highlights geologic events important to North Carolina and the rocks of Carl Sandburg Home National Historic Site. Geologic map units (see Geologic Map Data section) are listed in the center. Those with an * are mapped within the park. Red lines indicate major unconformities between eras. Radiometric ages shown are in millions of years (Ma). Graphic by Trista Thornberry-Ehrlich with information from the U.S. Geological Survey (http://pubs.usgs.gov/fs/2010/3059/) and the International Commission on Stratigraphy (http://www.stratigraphy.org/column.php?id=Chart/Time%20Scale).

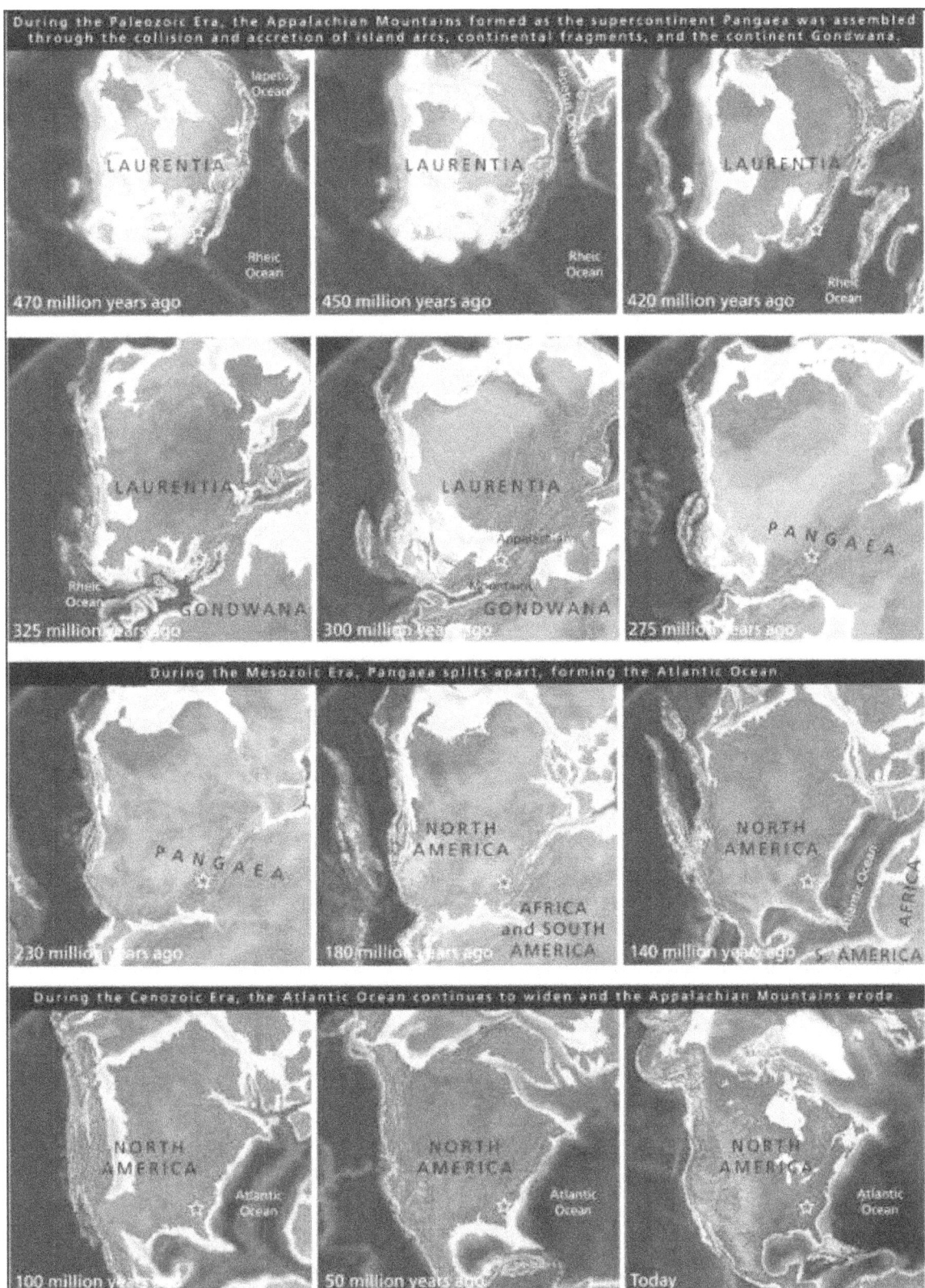

Figure 13. The bedrock geologic units of Carl Sandburg National Historic Site and surrounding area are tied to the intense deformation and intrusion of molten material during the formation of the Appalachian Mountains during several Paleozoic orogenies. Pangaea began to split apart during the Mesozoic and the Appalachian Mountains began to erode. Today, the Atlantic Ocean continues to widen and erosion has exposed the core of the Appalachian Mountains. Red stars indicate approximate location of Carl Sandburg Home National Historic Site. Graphic compiled by Jason Kenworthy (NPS Geologic Resources Division). Base paleogeographic maps by Ron Blakey (Colorado Plateau Geosystems, Inc.) are available online: http://cpgeosystems.com/paleomaps.html.

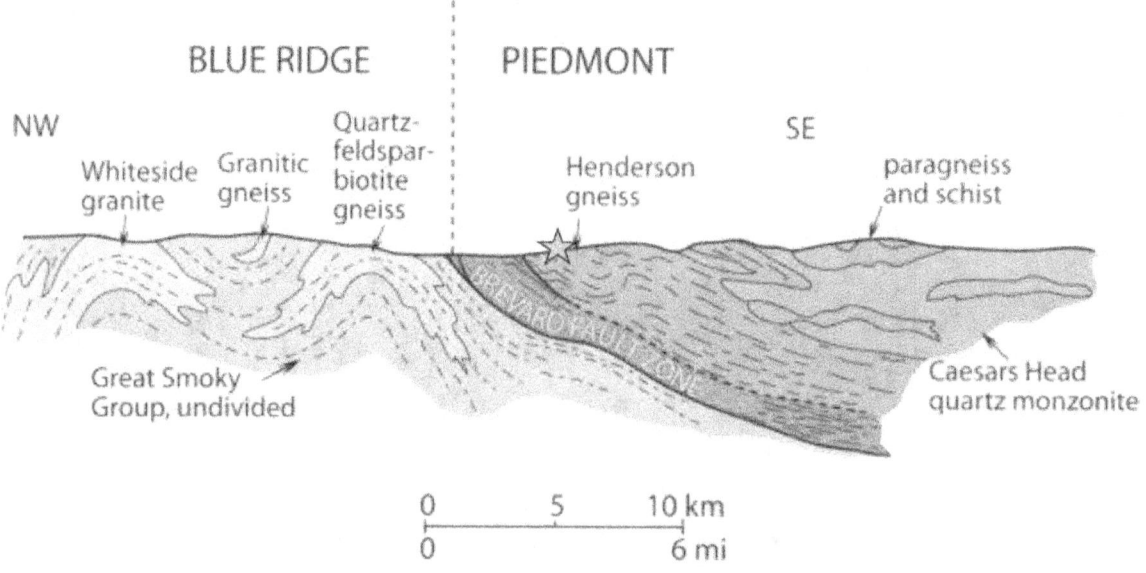

Figure 14. Cross sectional view of the Brevard Zone separating the Proterozoic rocks of the Blue Ridge from the Paleozoic rocks of the Piedmont in the vicinity of Carl Sandburg Home National Historic Site (location of which is denoted by green star). Adapted from Vauchez and Brunel (1988) by Trista L. Thornberry-Ehrlich (Colorado State University).

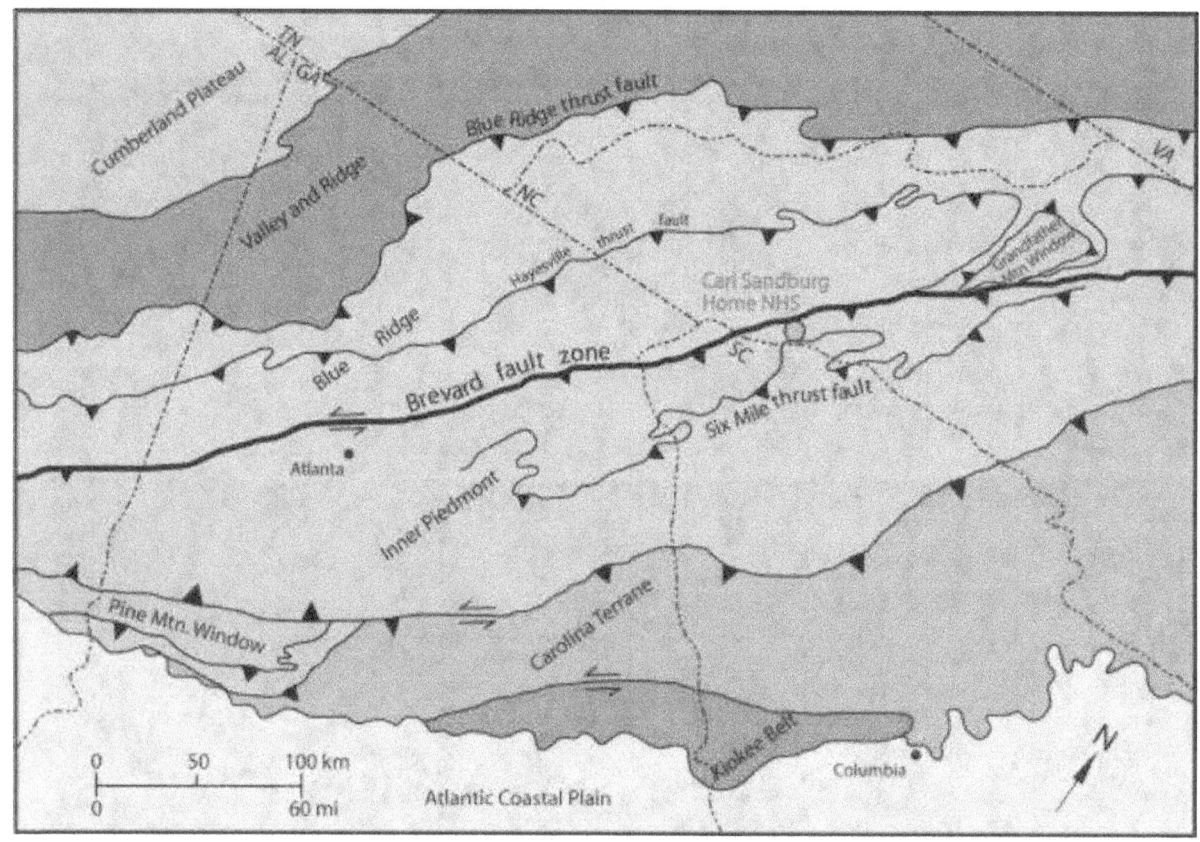

Figure 15. Map showing major tectonic units of part of the southern Appalachians in the vicinity of Carl Sandburg Home National Historic Site (location of which is denoted by green dot). Note the location of the Brevard fault zone, in particular. Triangular teeth denote the overriding block along thrust faults. Windows are areas where the overriding block eroded deep enough to exposure the underlying block. Adapted from figure 1-1 in Liu (1999) by Trista L. Thornberry-Ehrlich (Colorado State University).

Geologic Map Data

This section summarizes the geologic map data available for Carl Sandburg Home National Historic Site. It includes a fold-out geologic map overview and a summary table that lists each map unit displayed on the digital geologic map for the park. Complete GIS data are included on the accompanying CD and are also available at the Geologic Resources Inventory (GRI) publications website:
http://www.nature.nps.gov/geology/inventory/gre_publications.cfm.

Geologic Maps

Geologic maps facilitate an understanding of an area's geologic framework and the evolution of its present landscape. Using designated colors and symbols, geologic maps portray the spatial distribution and relationships of rocks and unconsolidated deposits. Geologic maps also may show geomorphic features, structural interpretations, and locations of past geologic hazards that may be prone to future activity. Additionally, anthropogenic features such as mines and quarries may be indicated on geologic maps.

Source Maps

The Geologic Resources Inventory (GRI) team converts digital and/or paper source maps into the GIS formats that conform to the GRI GIS data model. The GRI digital geologic map product also includes essential elements of the source maps, including unit descriptions, map legend, map notes, references, and figures. The GRI team used the following source maps to create the digital geologic data for Carl Sandburg Home National Historic Site:

Lemmon, R. E. 1978. Manuscript Geologic Map of the Hendersonville Quadrangle, North Carolina (scale 1:24,000). Unpublished. North Carolina Geological Survey, Raleigh, North Carolina, USA.

These source maps provided information for the "Geologic Issues," "Geologic Features and Processes," and "Geologic History" sections of this report.

Geologic GIS Data

The GRI team implements a GIS data model that standardizes map deliverables. The data model is included on the enclosed CD and is also available online (http://science.nature.nps.gov/im/inventory/geology/GeologyGISDataModel.cfm). This data model dictates GIS data structure including layer architecture, feature attribution, and relationships within ESRI ArcGIS software. The GRI team digitized the data for Carl Sandburg Home National Historic Site using data model version 2.1.

GRI digital geologic data for Carl Sandburg Home National Historic Site are included on the attached CD and are available through the NPS Integrated Resource Management Applications portal (https://irma.nps.gov/App/Portal/Home). Enter "GRI" as the search text and select Carl Sandburg Home National Historic Site from the unit list. The following components and geology data layers are part of the data set:

- Data in ESRI geodatabase and shapefile GIS formats
- Layer files with feature symbology
- Federal Geographic Data Committee (FGDC)–compliant metadata
- A map document (.pdf) that contains all of the ancillary map information and graphics, including geologic unit correlation tables and map unit descriptions, legends, and other information captured from source maps.
- An ESRI map document file (.mxd) that displays the digital geologic data

Table 2. Geology data layers in the Carl Sandburg Home National Historic Site GIS data.

Data Layer	Code	On Geologic Map Overview?
Geologic Attitude and Observation Points	ATD	Yes
Faults	FLT	Yes
Bedrock Contacts	GLGA	Yes
Bedrock Units	GLG	Yes
Linear Geologic Units	GLN	Yes
Surficial Units	SUR	Yes
Surficial Contacts	SURA	Yes

Geologic Map Overview

The geologic map overview (in pocket) displays the GRI digital geologic data draped over a shaded relief image of Carl Sandburg Home National Historic Site, and includes basic geographic information. The digital elevation data and geographic information are not included with the GRI digital geologic GIS data for the park, but are available online from a variety of sources.

Map Unit Properties Table

The geologic units listed on the map unit properties table (in pocket) correspond to the accompanying digital geologic data. Following the overall structure of the report, the table highlights the geologic issues, features, and processes associated with each map unit. The units, their relationships, and the series of events that created them are highlighted in the "Geologic History" section. Please refer to the geologic timescale (fig. 12) for the geologic period and age associated with each unit.

Use Constraints

Graphic and written information provided in this section are not a substitute for site-specific investigations, and ground-disturbing activities should neither be permitted nor denied based upon the information provided here. Minor inaccuracies may exist regarding the location of geologic features relative to other geologic or geographic features on the overview graphic. Based on the source map scale (1:24,000) and U.S. National Map Accuracy Standards, geologic features represented here are within 12 m (40 ft) (horizontally) of their true location.

Please contact GRI with any questions.

Glossary

This glossary contains brief definitions of technical geologic terms used in this report. Not all geologic terms used are referenced. For more detailed definitions or to find terms not listed here please visit: http://geomaps.wr.usgs.gov/parks/misc/glossarya.html. Definitions are based on those in the American Geological Institute Glossary of Geology *(fifth edition; 2005).*

absolute age. The geologic age of a fossil, rock, feature, or event in years; commonly refers to radiometrically determined ages.

accretion. The gradual addition of new land to old by the deposition of sediment or emplacement of landmasses onto the edge of a continent at a convergent margin.

accretionary prism. A wedge-shaped body of deformed rock consisting of material scraped off of subducting oceanic crust at a subduction zone. Accretionary prisms form in the same manner as a pile of snow in front of a snowplow.

active margin. A plate boundary where lithospheric plates come together (convergent boundary), pull apart (divergent boundary) or slide past one another (transform boundary). Typically associated with earthquakes and, in the case of convergent and divergent boundaries, volcanism. Compare to "passive margin."

alkalic. Describes rocks that are enriched in sodium and potassium.

allochthon. A mass of rock or fault block that has been moved from its place of origin by tectonic processes; commonly underlain by décollements.

allochthonous. Describes rocks or materials formed elsewhere and subsequently transported to their present location. Accreted terranes are one example.

alluvial fan. A fan-shaped deposit of sediment that accumulates where a hydraulically confined stream flows to a hydraulically unconfined area. Commonly out of a mountainous area into an area such as a valley or plain.

alluvium. Stream-deposited sediment.

amphibole. A common group of rock-forming silicate minerals. Hornblende is the most abundant type.

amphibolite. A metamorphic rock consisting mostly of the minerals amphibole and plagioclase with little or no quartz.

anticline. A convex-upward ("A" shaped) fold. Older rocks are found in the center.

anticlinorium. A large, regional feature with an overall shape of an anticline. Composed of many smaller folds.

aquifer. A rock or sedimentary unit that is sufficiently porous that it has a capacity to hold water, sufficiently permeable to allow water to move through it, and currently saturated to some level.

arc. See "volcanic arc" and "magmatic arc."

ash (volcanic). Fine material ejected from a volcano (also see "tuff").

asthenosphere. Earth's relatively weak layer or shell below the rigid lithosphere.

augen. Describes large lenticular mineral grains or mineral aggregates that have the shape of an eye in cross-section. Found in metamorphic rocks such as schists and gneisses.

authigenic. Describes rocks or minerals that have not been transported from where they formed.

autochthon. A body of rocks in the footwall (underlying side) of a fault that has not moved substantially from its site of origin. Although not moved, the rocks may be mildly to considerably deformed.

authochthonous. Formed or produced in the place where now found. Similar to "authigenic," which refers to constituents rather than whole formations.

axis (fold). A straight line approximation of the trend of a fold which divides the two limbs of the fold. "Hinge line" is a preferred term.

basalt. A dark-colored, often low-viscosity, extrusive igneous rock.

basement. The undifferentiated rocks, commonly igneous and metamorphic, that underlie rocks exposed at the surface.

basin (structural). A doubly plunging syncline in which rocks dip inward from all sides.

basin (sedimentary). Any depression, from continental to local scale, into which sediments are deposited.

batholith. A massive, discordant pluton, larger than 100 km^2 (40 mi^2), and often formed from multiple intrusions of magma.

bed. The smallest sedimentary strata unit, commonly ranging in thickness from one centimeter to a meter or two, and distinguishable from beds above and below.

bedding. Depositional layering or stratification of sediments.

bedrock. A general term for the rock that underlies soil or other unconsolidated, surficial material.

block (fault). A crustal unit bounded by faults, either completely or in part.

breccia. A coarse-grained, generally unsorted sedimentary rock consisting of cemented angular clasts greater than 2 mm (0.08 in).

brittle. Describes a rock that fractures (breaks) before sustaining deformation.

calcareous. Describes rock or sediment that contains the mineral calcium carbonate ($CaCO_3$).

calcite. A common rock-forming mineral: $CaCO_3$ (calcium carbonate).

carbonate. A mineral that has CO_3^{-2} as its essential component (e.g., calcite and aragonite).

carbonate rock. A rock consisting chiefly of carbonate minerals (e.g., limestone, dolomite, or carbonatite).

cataclastic. Describes structures in a rock such as bending, breaking, or crushing of minerals that result from extreme stresses during metamorphism.

cataclasite. A fine-grained rock formed by pervasive fracturing, milling, crushing, and grinding by brittle deformation, typically under high pressure.

cementation. Chemical precipitation of material into pores between grains, that binds the grains into rock.

chemical weathering. Chemical breakdown of minerals at Earth's surface via reaction with water, air, or dissolved substances; commonly results in a change in chemical composition more stable in the current environment.

clast. An individual grain or rock fragment in a sedimentary rock, produced by the physical disintegration of a larger rock mass.

clastic. Describes rock or sediment made of fragments of pre-existing rocks (clasts).

clay. Can be used to refer to clay minerals or as a sedimentary fragment size classification (less than 1/256 mm [0.00015 in]).

cleavage (mineral). The tendency of a mineral to break preferentially in certain directions along planes of weaknesses in the crystal structure.

cleavage. The tendency of a rock to split along parallel, closely spaced planar surfaces. It is independent of bedding.

clinopyroxene. A group name for pyroxene minerals crystallizing in the monoclinic system.

colluvium. A general term for any loose, heterogeneous, and incoherent mass of soil material and/or rock fragments deposited through the action of surface runoff (rainwash, sheetwash) or slow, continuous downslope creep.

concordant. Strata with contacts parallel to the orientation of adjacent strata.

conglomerate. A coarse-grained, generally unsorted, sedimentary rock consisting of cemented, rounded clasts larger than 2 mm (0.08 in).

contact metamorphism. Local processes of high-temperature metamorphism taking place in rocks at or near their contact with a body of molten material.

continental crust. Crustal rocks rich in silica and alumina that underlie the continents; ranging in thickness from 35 km (22 mi) to 60 km (37 mi) under mountain ranges.

convergent boundary. A plate boundary where two tectonic plates are colliding.

core. The central part of Earth, beginning at a depth of about 2,900 km (1,800 mi), probably consisting of iron-nickel alloy.

country rock. The rock surrounding an igneous intrusion or pluton. Also, the rock enclosing or traversed by a mineral deposit.

craton. The relatively old and geologically stable interior of a continent (also see "continental shield").

creep. The slow, imperceptible downslope movement of mineral, rock, and soil particles under gravity.

crinoid. A marine invertebrate (echinoderm) that uses a stalk to attach itself to a substrate. "Arms" are used to capture food. Rare today, they were very common in the Paleozoic. Crinoids are also called "sea lilies."

cross section. A graphical interpretation of geology, structure, and/or stratigraphy in the third (vertical) dimension, based on mapped and measured geological extents and attitudes depicted in a vertically oriented plane.

crust. Earth's outermost compositional shell, 10 to 40 km (6 to 25 mi) thick, consisting predominantly of relatively low-density silicate minerals (also see "oceanic crust" and "continental crust").

crystalline. Describes a regular, orderly, repeating geometric structural arrangement of atoms.

crystal structure. The orderly and repeated arrangement of atoms in a crystal.

debris flow. A moving mass of rock fragments, soil, and mud, in which more than half the particles are larger than sand size.

décollement. A large-displacement (kilometers to tens of kilometers), shallowly-dipping to sub-horizontal fault or shear zone.

deformation. A general term for the process of faulting, folding, and shearing of rocks as a result of various Earth forces such as compression (pushing together) and extension (pulling apart).

detachment fault. Synonym for décollement. Widely used for a regionally extensive, gently dipping normal fault that is commonly associated with extension in a metamorphic core complex.

diabase. An intrusive igneous rock consisting primarily of the minerals labradorite and pyroxene.

dike. A narrow igneous intrusion that cuts across bedding planes or other geologic structures.

dip. The angle between a bed or other geologic surface and horizontal.

dip-slip fault. A fault with measurable offset, where the relative movement is parallel to the dip of the fault.

disconformity. An unconformity where the bedding of the strata above and below are parallel.

divergent boundary. An active boundary where tectonic plates are moving apart (e.g., a spreading ridge or continental rift zone).

dolomite. A carbonate sedimentary rock of which more than 50% by weight or by areal percentages under the microscope consists of the mineral dolomite (calcium-magnesium carbonate).

dome. General term for any smoothly rounded landform or rock mass. More specifically, refers to an elliptical uplift in which rocks dip gently away in all directions.

downcutting. Stream erosion process in which the cutting is directed primarily downward, as opposed to lateral erosion.

drainage basin. The total area from which a stream system receives or drains precipitation runoff.

ductile. Describes a rock that is able to sustain deformation (folding, bending, or shearing) before fracturing.

entrainment. The process of picking up and transporting sediment, commonly by wind or water.

ephemeral stream. A stream that flows briefly only in direct response to precipitation in the immediate locality, and whose channel is at all times above the water table.

epicenter. The point on Earth's surface that is directly above the focus (location) of an earthquake.

escarpment. A steep cliff or topographic step resulting from vertical displacement on a fault or by mass movement. Also called a "scarp."

eustatic. Relates to simultaneous worldwide rise or fall of sea level.

exfoliation. The breakup, spalling, peeling, or flaking of layers or concentric sheets from an exposed rock mass caused by differential stresses due to thermal changes, or a reduction in pressure when overlying rocks erode away.

extension. A type of strain resulting from forces "pulling apart." Opposite of compression.

extrusive. Describes molten (igneous) material that has erupted onto Earth's surface.

facies (metamorphic). The pressure and temperature conditions that result in a particular, distinctive suite of metamorphic minerals.

fault. A break in rock along which relative movement has occurred between the two sides.

feldspar. A group of abundant (more than 60% of Earth's crust), light-colored to translucent silicate minerals found in all types of rocks. Usually white and gray to pink. May contain potassium, sodium, calcium, barium, rubidium, and strontium, along with aluminum, silica, and oxygen.

felsic. Describes an igneous rock having abundant light-colored minerals, such as quartz, feldspars, or muscovite. Compare to "mafic".

floodplain. The surface or strip of relatively smooth land adjacent to a river channel and formed by the river. Covered with water when the river overflows its banks.

fold. A curve or bend of an originally flat or planar structure, such as rock strata, bedding planes, or foliation, that is usually a product of deformation.

foliation. A preferred arrangement of crystal planes in minerals. In metamorphic rocks, the term commonly refers to a parallel orientation of planar minerals such as micas.

footwall. The mass of rock beneath a fault surface (also see "hanging wall").

formation. Fundamental rock-stratigraphic unit that is mappable, lithologically distinct from adjoining strata, and has definable upper and lower contacts.

fracture. Irregular breakage of a mineral; also any break in a rock (e.g., crack, joint, or fault).

fracture. Irregular breakage of a mineral. Any break in a rock (e.g., crack, joint, fault).

frost wedging. The breakup of rock due to the expansion of water freezing in fractures.

garnet. A hard mineral that has a glassy-luster, often with well defined crystal faces, and a variety of colors, dark red being characteristic. Commonly found in metamorphic rocks.

geology. The study of Earth including its origin, history, physical processes, components, and morphology.

gneiss. A foliated rock formed by regional metamorphism, with alternating bands of dark and light minerals.

granite. An intrusive igneous (plutonic) rock composed primarily of quartz and feldspar. Mica and amphibole minerals are also common. Intrusive equivalent of rhyolite.

graben. A down-dropped structural block bounded by steeply dipping, normal faults (also see "horst").

granodiorite. A group of intrusive igneous (plutonic) rocks containing quartz, plagioclase, and potassium feldspar minerals with biotite, hornblende, or, more rarely, pyroxene, as the mafic components.

greenschist. A metamorphic rock, whose green color is due to the presence of the minerals chlorite, epidote, or actinolite, corresponds with metamorphism at temperatures in the 300–500°C (570–930°F) range.

gully. A small channel produced by running water in earth or unconsolidated material (e.g., soil or a bare slope).

hanging wall. The mass of rock above a fault surface (also see "footwall").

hornblende. The most common mineral of the amphibole group. Hornblende is commonly black and occurs in distinct crystals, or in columnar, fibrous, or granular forms.

horst. Areas of relative "up" between grabens, representing the geologic surface left behind as grabens drop. The best example is the Basin-and-Range province of Nevada. The basins are grabens and the ranges are weathered horsts. Grabens become a locus for sedimentary deposition (also see "graben").

hydrogeologic. Refers to the geologic influences on groundwater and surface water composition, movement and distribution.

hydrolysis. A decomposition reaction involving water, frequently involving silicate minerals.

igneous. Refers to a rock or mineral that originated from molten material; one of the three main classes of rocks—igneous, metamorphic, and sedimentary.

intrusion. A body of igneous rock that invades (pushes into) older rock. The invading rock may be a plastic solid or magma.

island arc. A line or arc of volcanic islands formed over and parallel to a subduction zone.

isoclinal. Describes a fold with parallel limbs.

isotopic age. An age expressed in years and calculated from the quantitative determination of radioactive elements and their decay products; "absolute age" and "radiometric age" are often used in place of isotopic age but are less precise terms.

joint. A break in rock without relative movement of rocks on either side of the fracture surface.

laccolith. A mushroom- or arcuate-shaped pluton that has intruded sedimentary strata and domed up the overlying sedimentary layers. Common on the Colorado Plateau.

lacustrine. Pertaining to, produced by, or inhabiting a lake or lakes.

landslide. Any process or landform resulting from rapid, gravity-driven mass movement.

lava. Still-molten or solidified magma that has been extruded onto Earth's surface though a volcano or fissure.

left lateral fault. A strike-slip fault on which the side opposite the observer has been displaced to the left. Synonymous with "sinistral fault."

lens. A sedimentary deposit characterized by converging surfaces, thick in the middle and thinning out toward the edges, resembling a convex lens.

limb. Either side of a structural fold.

limestone. A sedimentary rock consisting chiefly of calcium carbonate, primarily in the form of the mineral calcite.

lineament. Any relatively straight surface feature that can be identified via observation, mapping, or remote sensing; often reflects crustal structure.

lithic. A sedimentary rock or pyroclastic deposit that contains abundant fragments of previously formed rocks.

lithification. The conversion of sediment into solid rock.

lithify. To change to stone or to petrify; especially to consolidate from a loose sediment to a solid rock, through compaction and cementation.

lithofacies. A lateral, mappable subdivision of a designated stratigraphic unit, distinguished from adjacent subdivisions on the basis of rock characteristics (lithology).

lithology. The physical description or classification of a rock or rock unit based on characteristics such as its color, mineral composition, and grain size.

lithosphere. The relatively rigid outmost shell of Earth's structure, 50 to 100 km (31 to 62 miles) thick, that encompasses the crust and uppermost mantle.

lithostratigraphy. The element of stratigraphy that deals with the lithology of strata, their organization into units based on lithologic characteristics, and their correlation.

mafic. Describes dark-colored rock, magma, or minerals rich in magnesium and iron. Compare to "felsic."

magma. Molten rock beneath Earth's surface capable of intrusion and extrusion.

magma reservoir. A chamber in the shallow part of the lithosphere from which volcanic materials are derived; the magma has ascended from a deeper source.

magmatic arc. Zone of plutons or volcanic rocks formed at a convergent boundary.

magmatism. The development and movement of magma, and its solidification to igneous rock.

mantle. The zone of Earth's interior between the crust and core.

mass wasting. A general term for the downslope movement of soil and rock material under the direct influence of gravity.

matrix. The fine-grained material between coarse (larger) grains in igneous rocks or poorly sorted clastic sediments or rocks. Also refers to rock or sediment in which a fossil is embedded.

mechanical weathering. The physical breakup of rocks without change in composition. Synonymous with "physical weathering."

mélange. A mappable body of jumbled rock that includes fragments and blocks of all sizes, both formed in place and those formed elsewhere, embedded in a fragmented and generally sheared matrix.

member. A lithostratigraphic unit with definable contacts; a member subdivides a formation.

meta–. A prefix used with the name of a sedimentary or igneous rock, indicating that the rock has been metamorphosed.

metamorphic. Describes the process of metamorphism or its results. One of the three main classes of rocks— igneous, metamorphic, and sedimentary.

metamorphic core complex. A generally domal or arch-like uplift of deformed metamorphic and plutonic rocks, overlain by tectonically detached and distended relatively unmetamorphosed cover rocks.

metamorphism. Literally, a change in form. Metamorphism occurs in rocks through mineral alteration, formation, and/or recrystallization from increased heat and/or pressure.

metavolcanic. An informal term for volcanic rocks that show evidence of metamorphism.

mica. A prominent rock-forming mineral of igneous and metamorphic rocks. It has perfect basal cleavage, meaning that it forms flat sheets.

migmatite. Literally, "mixed rock" with both igneous and metamorphic characteristics due to partial melting during metamorphism.

mineral. A naturally occurring, inorganic crystalline solid with a definite chemical composition or compositional range.

muscovite. A mineral of the mica group. It is colorless to pale brown, and is a common mineral in metamorphic rocks such as gneiss and schist, igneous rocks such as granite, pegmatite, and sedimentary rocks such as sandstone.

mylonite. A fine-grained, foliated rock typically found in localized zones of ductile deformation, often formed at great depths under high temperature and pressure.

mylonite structure. A flow-like appearance, characteristic of mylonites, that is produced by intense, small-scale crushing, breaking, and shearing of the rock.

nappe. A sheetlike, allochthonous (manufactured elsewhere) rock unit that has moved along a predominantly horizontal surface. The mechanism may be thrust faulting, recumbent folding, or gravity sliding.

nonconformity. An erosional surface preserved in strata in which crystalline igneous or metamorphic rocks underlie sedimentary rocks.

normal fault. A dip-slip fault in which the hanging wall moves down relative to the footwall.

obduction. The process by which the crust is thickened by thrust faulting at a convergent margin.

oblique fault. A fault in which motion includes both dip-slip and strike-slip components (also see "dip-slip fault" and "strike-slip fault").

oceanic crust. Earth's crust formed at spreading ridges that underlies the ocean basins. Oceanic crust is 6 to 7 km (3 to 4 miles) thick and generally of basaltic composition.

olivine. An olive-green mineral rich in iron, magnesium, and manganese that is commonly found in low-silica (basaltic) igneous rocks.

orogeny. A mountain-building event.

outcrop. Any part of a rock mass or formation that is exposed or "crops out" at Earth's surface.

overbank deposit. Alluvium deposited outside a stream channel during flooding.

overburden. Rock and sediment, not of economic value, and often unconsolidated, that overlies an ore, fuel, or sedimentary deposit.

paleogeography. The study, description, and reconstruction of the physical landscape from past geologic periods.

paleontology. The study of the life and chronology of Earth's geologic past based on the fossil record.

Pangaea. A theoretical, single supercontinent that existed during the Permian and Triassic periods.

parent material. Geologic material from which soils form.

parent rock. Rock from which soil, sediments, or other rocks are derived.

passive margin. A margin where no plate-scale tectonism is taking place; plates are not converging, diverging, or sliding past one another. An example is the east coast of North America. (also see "active margin").

permeability. A measure of the relative ease with which fluids move through the pore spaces of rocks or sediments.

phenocryst. A coarse (large) crystal in a porphyritic igneous rock.

phreatic zone. The zone of saturation. Phreatic water is groundwater.

phyllite. A metamorphosed rock, intermediate in grade between slate and mica schist, with minute crystals of graphite, sericite, or chlorite that impart a silky sheen to the surfaces ("schistosity").

plastic. Capable of being deformed permanently without rupture.

plate tectonics. The concept that the lithosphere is broken up into a series of rigid plates that move over Earth's surface above a more fluid asthenosphere.

plateau. A broad, flat-topped topographic high (terrestrial or marine) of great extent and elevation above the surrounding plains, canyons, or valleys.

plume. A persistent, pipe-like body of hot material moving upward from Earth's mantle into the crust.

pluton (plutonic). A body of intrusive igneous rock that crystallized at some depth beneath Earth's surface.

porosity. The proportion of void space (e.g., pores or voids) in a volume of rock or sediment deposit.

potassium feldspar. A feldspar mineral rich in potassium (e.g., orthoclase, microcline, sanidine, adularia).

protolith. The parent or unweathered and/or unmetamorphosed rock from which regolith or metamorphosed rock is formed.

pull-apart basin. A topographic depression created by an extensional bend or extensional overstep along a strike-slip fault.

pyroxene. A common rock-forming mineral. It is characterized by short, stout crystals.

quartzite. Metamorphosed quartz sandstone.

radioactivity. The spontaneous decay or breakdown of unstable atomic nuclei.

radiometric age. An age expressed in years and calculated from the quantitative determination of radioactive elements and their decay products.

recharge. Infiltration processes that replenish groundwater.

regolith. General term for the layer of rock debris, organic matter, and soil that commonly forms the land surface and overlies most bedrock.

regression. A long-term seaward retreat of the shoreline, or relative fall of sea level.

relative dating. Determining the chronological placement of rocks, events, or fossils with respect to the geologic time scale, and without reference to their numerical age.

reverse fault. A contractional high-angle (greater than 45°) dip-slip fault in which the hanging wall moves up relative to the footwall (also see "thrust fault").

rift. A region of crust where extension results in formation of many related normal faults, often associated with volcanic activity.

rift valley. A depression formed by grabens along the crest of an oceanic spreading ridge or in a continental rift zone.

rock. A solid, cohesive aggregate of one or more minerals.

rock fall. Mass wasting process where rocks are dislodged and move downslope rapidly; it is the fastest mass wasting process.

sand. A clastic particle smaller than a granule and larger than a silt grain, having a diameter in the range of 1/16 mm (0.0025 in) to 2 mm (0.08 in).

sandstone. Clastic sedimentary rock of predominantly sand-sized grains.

saprolite. Soft, often clay-rich, decomposed rock formed in place by chemical weathering.

scarp. A steep cliff or topographic step resulting from displacement on a fault, or by mass movement, or erosion. Also called an "escarpment."

schist. A strongly foliated metamorphic rock that can be readily split into thick flakes or slabs. Micas are arranged in parallel, imparting a distinctive sheen, or "schistosity" to the rock.

schistose. A rock displaying schistosity, or foliation.

seafloor spreading. The process by which tectonic plates pull apart and new lithosphere is created at oceanic ridges.

sediment. An eroded and deposited, unconsolidated accumulation of rock and mineral fragments.

sedimentary rock. A consolidated and lithified rock consisting of clastic and/or chemical sediment(s). One of the three main classes of rocks—igneous, metamorphic, and sedimentary.

sequence. A major informal rock-stratigraphic unit that is traceable over large areas, and defined by sediments associated with a major sea level transgression-regression.

shale. A clastic sedimentary rock made of clay-sized particles that exhibit parallel splitting properties.

shear zone. A zone of rock that has been crushed and brecciated by many parallel fractures due to shear strain.

silicate. A compound whose crystal structure contains the SiO_4 tetrahedra.

sill. An igneous intrusion that is of the same orientation as the surrounding rock.

silt. Clastic sedimentary material intermediate in size between fine-grained sand and coarse clay (1/256 to 1/16 mm [0.00015 to 0.002 in]).

siltstone. A variably lithified sedimentary rock composed of silt-sized grains.

slope. The inclined surface of any geomorphic feature or measurement thereof. Synonymous with "gradient."

slump. A generally large, coherent mass movement with a concave-up failure surface and subsequent backward rotation relative to the slope.

soil. Surface accumulation of weathered rock and organic matter capable of supporting plant growth, and often overlying the parent material from which it formed.

soliflucation. The slow downslope movement of waterlogged soil, normally at 0.5–5.0 cm/year (0.2–2 in/year), especially the flow occurring at high elevations in regions underlain by frozen ground. that acts as a downward barrier to water percolation, initiated by frost action and augmented by meltwater resulting from alternate freezing and thawing of snow and ground ice.

speleothem. Any secondary mineral deposit that forms in a cave.

spreading center. A divergent boundary where two lithospheric plates are spreading apart. It is a source of new crustal material.

spring. A site where water issues from the surface due to the intersection of the water table with the ground surface.

stock. An igneous intrusion exposed at the surface; less than 100 km^2 (40 mi^2) in size. Compare to "pluton."

strata. Tabular or sheet-like masses or distinct layers of rock.

stratification. The accumulation, or layering of sedimentary rocks in strata. Tabular, or planar, stratification refers to essentially parallel surfaces. Cross-stratification refers to strata inclined at an angle to the main stratification.

stratigraphy. The geologic study of the origin, occurrence, distribution, classification, correlation, and age of rock layers, especially sedimentary rocks.

stream. Any body of water moving under gravity flow in a clearly confined channel.

stream channel. A long, narrow depression shaped by the concentrated flow of a stream and covered continuously or periodically by water.

stream terrace. Step-like benches surrounding the present floodplain of a stream due to dissection of previous flood plain(s), stream bed(s), and/or valley floor(s).

strike. The compass direction of the line of intersection of an inclined surface with a horizontal plane.

strike-slip fault. A fault with measurable offset where the relative movement is parallel to the strike of the fault. Said to be "sinistral" (left-lateral) if relative motion of the block opposite the observer appears to be to the left. "Dextral" (right-lateral) describes relative motion to the right.

structural geology. The branch of geology that deals with the description, representation, and analysis of structures, chiefly on a moderate to small scale. The subject is similar to tectonics, but the latter is generally used for the broader regional or historical phases.

structure. The attitude and relative positions of the rock masses of an area resulting from such processes as faulting, folding, and igneous intrusions.

subduction zone. A convergent plate boundary where oceanic lithosphere descends beneath a continental or oceanic plate and is carried down into the mantle.

subsidence. The gradual sinking or depression of part of Earth's surface.

suture. The linear zone where two continental landmasses become joined via obduction.

syncline. A downward curving (concave up) fold with layers that dip inward; the core of the syncline contains the stratigraphically-younger rocks.

synclinorium. A composite synclinal structure of regional extent composed of lesser folds.

system (stratigraphy). The group of rocks formed during a period of geologic time.

talus. Rock fragments, usually coarse and angular, lying at the base of a cliff or steep slope from which they have been derived.

tectonic. Relating to large-scale movement and deformation of Earth's crust.

tectonics. The geologic study of the broad structural architecture and deformational processes of the lithosphere and asthenosphere.

terrace. A relatively level bench or steplike surface, breaking the continuity of a slope (see "marine terrace" and "stream terrace").

terrane. A large region or group of rocks with similar geology, age, or structural style.

terrestrial. Relating to land, Earth, or its inhabitants.

terrigenous. Derived from the land or a continent.

thrust fault. A contractional dip-slip fault with a shallowly dipping fault surface (less than 45°) where the hanging wall moves up and over relative to the footwall.

topography. The general morphology of Earth's surface, including relief and locations of natural and anthropogenic features.

tourmaline. A crystal silicate mineral occurring in three-, six-, or nine-sided prisms, composed of elements such as sodium, calcium, magnesium, iron, aluminum, lithium, and sometime fluorine in small amounts. Tourmaline is classed as a semi-precious stone and the gem comes in a wide variety of colors.

trace (fault). The exposed intersection of a fault with Earth's surface.

transcurrent fault. A term for a continental strike-slip fault that does not terminate at lithospheric plate boundaries.

transform fault. A strike-slip fault that links two other faults or two other plate boundaries (e.g. two segments of a mid-ocean ridge). A type of plate boundary at which lithosphere is neither created nor destroyed, and plates slide past each other on a strike-slip fault.

transgression. Landward migration of the sea as a result of a relative rise in sea level.

transpression. A system of stresses that tends to cause oblique shortening (combined shortening and strike-slip).

transpressional fault. A strike-slip fault across which there is a component of shortening.

trend. The direction or azimuth of elongation of a linear geologic feature.

turbidite. A sediment or rock deposited from a turbidity current (underwater flow of sediment) and characterized by graded bedding, moderate sorting, and well-developed primary structures in the sequence noted in the Bouma cycle.

type locality. The geographic location where a stratigraphic unit (or fossil) is well displayed, formally defined, and derives its name. The place of original description.

ultramafic. Describes rock composed chiefly of mafic (dark-colored, iron and magnesium rich) minerals.

unconfined groundwater. Groundwater that has a water table; i.e., water not confined under pressure beneath a confining bed.

unconformity. An erosional or non-depositional surface bounded on one or both sides by sedimentary strata. An unconformity marks a period of missing time.

undercutting. The removal of material at the base of a steep slope or cliff or other exposed rock by the erosive action of falling or running water (such as a meandering stream), of sand-laden wind in the desert, or of waves along the coast.

uplift. A structurally high area in the crust, produced by movement that raises the rocks.

vadose water. Water of the unsaturated zone or zone of aeration.

volcanic. Describes anything related to volcanoes. Can refer to igneous rock crystallized at or near Earth's surface (e.g., lava).

volcanic arc. A commonly curved, linear, zone of volcanoes above a subduction zone.

volcaniclastic. Describes clastic volcanic materials formed by any process of fragmentation, dispersed by any kind of transporting agent, deposited in any environment.

volcanogenic. Describes material formed by volcanic processes.

water table. The upper surface of the saturated zone; the zone of rock in an aquifer saturated with water.

weathering. The physical, chemical, and biological processes by which rock is broken down.

xenolith. A rock particle, formed elsewhere, entrained in magma as an inclusion.

zircon. A common accessory mineral in siliceous igneous rocks, crystalline limestone, schist, and gneiss, also in sedimentary rocks derived from and in beach and river placer deposits. When cut and polished, the colorless varieties provide exceptionally brilliant gemstones. Very durable mineral, often used for age-dating.

Literature Cited

This section lists references cited in this report. A more complete geologic bibliography is available from the National Park Service Geologic Resources Division.

Alfano, J. A., Jr. 1993. Hydrogeological evaluation of a fractured crystalline rock aquifer, Hendersonville, North Carolina. Thesis. Georgia State University, Atlanta, Georgia, USA.

Bier, S. E., B. R. Bream, and R. D. Hatcher, Jr. 2000. Detailed geologic mapping of the western and central inner Piedmont, North Carolina. Geological Society of America Abstracts with Programs 32(7):234.

Braile, L.W. 2009. Seismic monitoring. Pages 229–244 in R. Young, R. and L. Norby, editors. Geological Monitoring. Geological Society of America, Boulder, Colorado, USA. http://nature.nps.gov/geology/monitoring/seismic.cfm. Accessed 4 August 2011.

Bream, B. R., R. D. Hatcher, Jr., and J. C. Hill. 1998. The Henderson augen gneiss of the western Inner Piedmont, NC & SC. Geological Society of America Abstracts with Programs 30(7):125.

Beutel, E., S. Jaume, B. Doyle, and N. Levine. 2008. South Carolina Earthquake Education and Preparedness Hazard Professional Workshop. http://scearthquakes.cofc.edu/support_files/EKB_SCE MD_workshop.pdf. Accessed 4 August 2011.

Butler, J. R., and D. T. Secor, Jr. 1991. The central Piedmont. Pages 59–78 in J. W. Horton, Jr. and V. A. Zullo, editors. The Geology of the Carolinas: Carolina Geological society fiftieth anniversary volume. University of Tennessee Press, Knoxville, Tennessee, USA.

Clark, S. H. B. 2001. Birth of the mountains; the geologic story of the Southern Appalachian Mountains. U.S. Geological Survey, Reston, Virginia, USA. General Interest Publication. http://pubs.usgs.gov/gip/birth/. Accessed 4 August 2011.

Connelly, J. B. and N. B. Woodward. 1990. Sequential restoration of early Paleozoic deformation; Great Smoky Mountain foothills, Tennessee. Geological Society of America Abstracts with Programs 22(4):8.

Connelly, J. B. and N. B. Woodward. 1992. Taconian foreland-style thrust system in the Great Smoky Mountains, Tennessee. Geology 20(2):177–180.

Connors, T. 2000. Geologic Resources Inventory Workshop Summary-Great Smoky Mountain National Park. NPS Geologic Resources Division, Denver, Colorado, USA. http://www.nature.nps.gov/geology/inventory/publica tions/s_summaries/GRSM_scoping_summary_200007 24.pdf. Accessed 4 August 2011.

Davis, T. L. 1993. Lithostratigraphy, structure, and metamorphism of a crystalline thrust terrane, western Inner Piedmont, North Carolina. Dissertation. University of Tennessee at Knoxville, Knoxville, Tennessee, USA.

Denver Service Center. 1998. Rapid Visual Screening of Buildings for Potential Seismic Hazards at Carl Sandburg Home National Historic Site, Cowpens National Battlefield, Kings Mountain National Military Park. NPS Document 445/D-27. National Park Service, Denver, Colorado, USA.

Department of Environment and Natural Resources. 2010. North Carolina Ecosystem Response to Climate Change. DENR Assessment of Effects and Adaptation Measures (draft). Raleigh, North Carolina, USA. http://www.climatechange.nc.gov/pages/ClimateChan ge/Climate_Change_Ecosystem_Assessment_Summary .pdf. Accessed 4 August 2011.

DeWindt, J.T. 1975. Geology of the Great Smoky Mountains, Tennessee and North Carolina, with road log for field excursion, Knoxville-Clingmans Dome-Maryville. Compass of Sigma Gamma Epsilon 1915-84 52(4):73–129.

EarthScope.org. 2011. Seismic and Magnetotelluric Array (USArray). http://www.earthscope.org/observatories/usarray. Accessed 4 August 2011.

Garihan, J. M. and C. W. Clendenin. 2007. The Eastatoee Fault; recognition of a regional thrust-sheet bounding fault in the inner Piedmont thrust stack of northwestern South Carolina and western North Carolina. Geological Society of America Abstracts with Programs 39(2)11.

Garihan, J. M. 2002. Geology of the Standingstone Mountain 7.5-minute quadrangle, Inner Piedmont, North Carolina and South Carolina. Geological Society of America Abstracts with Programs 34(2):11.

Garihan, J. M., M. S. Preddy, and W. A. Ransom. 1993. Summary of mid-Mesozoic brittle faulting in the Inner Piedmont and nearby Charlotte Belt of the Carolinas. Pages 55–65 in Studies of inner piedmont geology with a focus on the Columbus Promontory. Carolina Geological Society Annual Field Trip Guidebook. Carolina Geological Society, Durham, North Carolina, USA.

Garner, T., C. Luneburg, M. Schmocker, and H. Lebit. 2001. Structures and microstructures along the Brevard fault zone. Geological Society of America Abstracts with Programs 33(6):148.

Giorgis, S. D. 1999. Geology of the northwestern South Mountains near Morganton, North Carolina. Thesis. University of Tennessee at Knoxville, Knoxville, Tennessee, USA.

Giorgis, S. D. and R. D. Hatcher, Jr. 1999. Suspect Henderson augen gneiss contact relationships in the western Inner Piedmont, NC. Geological Society of America Abstracts with Programs 31(3):17.

Goldberg, S. A. and P. D. Fullagar. 1993. Alleghanian Rb-Sr mineral ages from the Inner Piedmont of southwestern North Carolina. Pages 105–107 in R.D. Hatcher, Jr. and T. L. Davis, editors. Studies of Inner Piedmont geology with a focus on the Columbus Promontory. Carolina Geological Society.

Goldsmith, R. G. 1981. Structural patterns in the Inner Piedmont of the Charlotte and Winston-Salem 2° quadrangles, North Carolina and South Carolina. Pages 19–27 in J. W. Horton, Jr., J. R. Butler, and D. M. Milton, editors. Geological investigations of the Kings Mountain belt and adjacent areas in the Carolinas. Carolina Geological Society Field Trip Guidebook 1981. South Carolina Geological Survey, Columbia, South Carolina, USA.

Goldstein, A. G.; Brown, L. L. 1985, Evolution of magnetic fabric in the Henderson Gneiss and Brevard Zone, North Carolina. Eos, Transactions, American Geophysical Union 66(18):252.

Harper, S. B., J. W. Roberts, and P. D. Fullagar, P. D. 1977. Geochronology of granitic gneisses of the inner Piedmont, northwestern North Carolina. Geological Society of America Abstracts with Programs 9(2):144.

Hart, S. 1993. Carl Sandburg Home National Historic Site Cultural Landscape Report. Cultural Resources Planning Division, Southeast Regional Office, National Park Service, U.S. Department of Interior. U.S. Government Printing Office.

Hatcher, R. D. Jr. 1993. Perspective on the tectonics of the Inner Piedmont, southern Appalachians. Pages 17–43 in R. D. Hatcher Jr. and T. L. Davis, editors. Studies of the Inner Piedmont geology with a focus on the Columbus Promontory. Carolina Geological Society Guidebook.

Hatcher, R. D., Jr., T. L. Davis, and G. M. Yanagihara. 1994. Structure of the Appalachian Inner Piedmont and eastern Blue Ridge. Geological Society of America Abstracts with Programs 26(4):18.

Hibbard, J. 2000. Docking Carolina; mid-Paleozoic accretion in the Southern Appalachians. Geology 28(2):127–130.

Hibbard, J. P., E. R. Stoddard, D. T. Secor, and A. J. Dennis. 2002. The Carolina Zone; overview of Neoproterozoic to early Paleozoic peri-Gondwanan terranes along the eastern flank of the Southern Appalachians. Earth-Science Reviews 57(3–4):299–339.

Hill, J. C. 1999. Stratigraphy, structure, and tectonics of the part of the Southern Appalachian inner Piedmont, near Marion, North Carolina. Thesis. University of Tennessee at Knoxville, Knoxville, Tennessee, USA.

Horton, J. W., Jr. 2006. Geologic map of the Kings Mountain and Grover quadrangles, Cleveland and Gaston Counties, North Carolina, and Cherokee and York Counties, South Carolina (scale 1:24,000). Open-File Report OF 2006-1238. U.S. Geological Survey, Reston, Virginia, USA.

Horton, J. W., Jr. 2008. Geologic map of the Kings Mountain and Grover quadrangles, Cleveland and Gaston Counties, North Carolina, and Cherokee and York Counties, South Carolina, (scale 1:24,000). Scientific Investigations Map 2981. U.S. Geological Survey, Reston, Virginia, USA.

Horton, J. W., Jr., A. A. Drake, and D. W. Rankin. 1994. Terranes and overlap sequences in the Central and Southern Appalachians, an expanded explanation for part of the Circum-Atlantic terrane map. Open-File Report OF 94-0682. U.S. Geological Survey, Reston, Virginia, USA.

Horton, J. W., Jr., A. A. Drake, D. W. Rankin, and R. D. Dallmeyer. 1988. Preliminary tectonostratigraphic terrane map of the central and southern Appalachian Orogen. Geological Society of America Abstracts with Programs 20(7): 23–124.

Horton, J. W., Jr., A. A. Drake, Jr., and D. W. Rankin. 1989a. Interpretation of tectonostratigraphic terranes in central and southern Appalachian Orogen, USA. International Geological Congress Abstracts 28(2):2.73–2.74.

Horton, J. W., Jr., A. A. Drake, Jr., and D. W. Rankin. 1989b. Tectonostratigraphic terranes and their Paleozoic boundaries in the Central and Southern Appalachians. Pages 213–245 in R. D. Dallmeyer, editor. Terranes in the circum-Atlantic Paleozoic orogens. Geological Society of America Special Paper 230. Geological Society of America, Boulder, Colorado, USA.

Horton, J. W., Jr. and V. A. Zullo. 1991. An introduction to the geology of the Carolinas. Pages 1–10 in J. W. Horton, Jr. and V. A. Zullo, editors. The geology of the Carolinas: Carolina Geological Society fiftieth anniversary volume. University of Tennessee Press, Knoxville, Tennessee, USA.

Houle, G. 1990. Species-area relationship during primary succession in granite outcrop plant communities. American Journal of Botany 77:1433-1439.

Howard, C. S. 2004. Geologic Map of the Kings Creek 7.5-minute quadrangle, Cherokee and York Counties (scale 1:24,000). Geologic Quadrangle Map GQM-16. South Carolina Geological Survey, Columbia, South Carolina, USA.

Hunt-Foster, R., J. P. Kenworthy, V. L. Santucci, T. Connors, and T. L. Thornberry-Ehrlich. 2009. Paleontological resource inventory and monitoring— Cumberland Piedmont Network. Natural Resource Technical Report NPS/NRPC/NRR—2009/235. National Park Service, Fort Collins, Colorado, USA.

Johnson, J .E. 2003. Forest Management Plan for the Carl Sandburg Home National Historic Site Flat Rock, North Carolina. Department of Forestry, Virginia Polytechnic Institute and State University, Blacksburg, Virginia, USA.

Jones, T. H. 2005. Historic Structure Report Connemara Main House Carl Sandburg Home National Historic Site, Flat Rock, NC. LCS# 05146. Cultural Resources Division, Historical Architecture, Southeast Regional Office, National Park Service, U.S. Department of Interior, Atlanta, Georgia, USA.

Keith, A. 1905. Description of the Mount Mitchell quadrangle , North Carolina-Tennessee. Geologic Atlas, Folio 124. U.S. Geological Survey, Reston, Virginia, USA.

Kenworthy, J. P. and V. L. Santucci. 2006. A Preliminary Inventory of National Park Service Paleontological Resources in Cultural Resource Contexts, Part 1: General Overview. Pages 70—76 in S. G. Lucas, J. A. Spielman, P. M. Hester, J. P. Kenworthy, and V. L. Santucci, editors. Fossils from Federal Lands. New Mexico Museum of Natural History and Science Bulletin 34. http://nature.nps.gov/geology/ paleontology/conf7articles.cfm. Accessed 4 August 2011.

King, P. B. 1955. A geologic section across the southern Appalachians: an outline of the geology in the segment in Tennessee, North Carolina, and South Caroline. Pages 332–373 in R. J. Russell, editor. Guide to southeastern geology. New York, New York, USA.

LeHuray, A. P. 1986. Isotopic evidence for a tectonic boundary between the Kings Mountain and Inner Piedmont belts, Southern Appalachians. Geology 14(9):784–787.

Lemmon, R. E. 1978. Manuscript Geologic Map of the Hendersonville Quadrangle, North Carolina (scale 1:24,000). Unpublished. North Carolina Geological Survey, Raleigh, North Carolina, USA.

Lemmon, R.E. 1981. An igneous origin for the Henderson augen gneiss, western North Carolina: evidence from zircon morphology. Southeastern Geology 22(2):79–90.

Liu, A. 1991. Structural geology and deformation history of the Brevard fault zone, Chauga Belt, and inner Piedmont, northwestern South Carolina and adjacent areas. Dissertation. University of Tennessee at Knoxville, Knoxville, Tennessee, USA.

Lord, M. L., D. Germanoski, and N. E. Allmendinger. 2009. Fluvial geomorphology: Monitoring stream systems in response to a changing environment. Pages 69–103 in R. Young and L. Norby, editors. Geological Monitoring. Geological Society of America, Boulder, Colorado, USA. http://nature.nps.gov/geology/monitoring/fluvial.cfm. Accessed 4 August 2011.

McDaniel, L. 2000. Longstreet Highroad Guide to the North Carolina Mountains, The Balsam Mountains. Sherpa Guides. http://sherpaguides.com/north_carolina/mountains/ba lsam_mountains/. Accessed 11 May 2011.

Meiman, J. 2005. Cumberland Piedmont Network Water Quality Report, February 2005, Carl Sandburg Home National Historic Site. NPS internal document.

Meiman, J. 2007. Cumberland Piedmont Network Water Quality Report, Carl Sandburg Home National Historic Site. Natural Resource Report NPS/SER/CUPN/NRTR—2007/001. Southeast Regional Office, National Park Service, Atlanta, Georgia, USA.

Meiman, J. 2008. Cumberland Piedmont Network Water Quality Report; Third Serial, Carl Sandburg Home National Historic Site. Natural Resource Report NPS/SER/CUPN/NRTR—2008/001. Southeast Regional Office, National Park Service, Atlanta, Georgia, USA.

Mitsch, W. J. and J. G. Gosselink. 1993. Wetlands (2nd edition). Van Nostrand Reinhold Company, New York, New York, USA.

Moore, H. L. 1988. A roadside guide to the geology of the Great Smoky Mountains National Park. University of Tennessee Press, Knoxville, Tennessee, USA.

Nance, R. D. and U. Linnemann. 2008. The Rheic Ocean; origin, evolution, and significance. GSA Today 18(12):4–12.

National Park Service. 2011. Nature and Science. Carl Sandburg Home National Historic Site. http://www.nps.gov/carl/naturescience/index.htm. Accessed 6 May 2011.

Nelson, A. E. 1981. Polydeformed rocks of the Lowndesville shear zone in the Greenville 2° quadrangle, South Carolina and Georgia. In Geological investigations of the Kings Mountain belt and adjacent areas in the Carolinas. Pages 175–193 in J. W. Horton, Jr., J. R. Butler, and D. M. Milton, editors. Carolina Geological Society Field Trip Guidebook 1981. South Carolina Geological Survey, Columbia, South Carolina, USA.

North Carolina Geological Survey. 1989. A Geologic Guide to North Carolina's State Parks. Bulletin 91. P. Albert Carpenter, III, editor. North Carolina Geological Survey Section, Division of Land Resources, Department of Natural Resources and Community Development, Raleigh, North Carolina, USA.

Nystrom, P G. Jr. 2003. Geologic Map of the Filbert 7.5-minute quadrangle, York County, South Carolina (scale 1:24,000). Geologic Quadrangle Map GQM-25. South Carolina Geological Survey, Columbia, South Carolina, USA.

Odom, A. L.; Fullagar, P.D. 1973. Geochronologic and tectonic relationships between the Inner Piedmont, Brevard Zone, and Blue Ridge belts, North Carolina. American Journal of Science 273-A:133–149.

Petersen, M. D., A. D. Frankel, S. C. Harmsen, C. S. Mueller, K. M. Haller, R. L. Wheeler, R. L. Wesson, Y. Zeng, O. S. Boyd, D. M. Perkins, N. Luco, E. H. Field, C. J. Wills, and K. S. Rukstales. 2008a. 2008 United States National Seismic Hazard Maps. Fact Sheet 2008-3018. U.S. Geological Survey, Reston, Virginia, USA. http://pubs.usgs.gov/fs/2008/3018/. Accessed 30 December 2010.

Petersen, M. D., A. D. Frankel, S. C. Harmsen, C. S. Mueller, K. M. Haller, R. L. Wheeler, R. L. Wesson, Y. Zeng, O. S. Boyd, D. M. Perkins, N. Luco, E. H. Field, C. J. Wills, and K. S. Rukstales. 2008b. Documentation for the 2008 Update of the United States National Seismic Hazard Maps. Open-File Report 2008-1128. U.S. Geological Survey, Reston, Virginia, USA. http://pubs.usgs.gov/of/2008/1128/. Accessed 31 December 2010.

Pittillo, J. D., G. A. Smathers, P. A. Delcourt, and H. R. Delcourt. 1980. Development of vegetational patterns during the late Pleistocene in the Southern Appalachian Balsam Mountains. Journal of the Elisha Mitchell Scientific Society 96(2):95–96.

Prowell, D. C., and S. F. Obermeier. 1991. Evidence of Cenozoic Tectonism. Pages 309–318 in J. W. Horton, Jr. and V. A. Zullo, editors. The geology of the Carolinas: Carolina Geological Society fiftieth anniversary volume. University of Tennessee Press, Knoxville, Tennessee, USA.

Ranson, W. A., I. S. Williams, and J. M. Garihan. 1999. SHRIMP zircon U-Pb ages of granitoids from the Inner Piedmont of South Carolina; evidence for Ordovician magmatism involving mid to late Proterozoic crust. Geological Society of America Abstracts with Programs 31(7):167.

Reed, J. C., Jr., Sigafoos, R. S., and Fisher, G. W. 1980. The River and the Rocks-The Geologic story of Great Falls and the Potomac River Gorge. U.S. Geological Survey Bulletin 1471. U.S. Geological Survey, Reston, Virginia, USA.

Rozen, R. W. 1981. The Middleton-Lowndesville cataclastic zone in the Elberton East quadrangle, Georgia. Pages 174–180 in J. W. Horton, Jr., J. R. Butler, and D. M. Milton, editors. Carolina Geological Society Field Trip Guidebook 1981. South Carolina Geological Survey, Columbia, South Carolina, USA.

Schaeffer, M. F. 1982. Polyphase deformation in the Kings Mountain Belt of North-central South Carolina and its implications for Southern Appalachian tectonic models. Geological Society of America Abstracts with Programs 14(1–2):80.

Schafale M. P. and A .S. Weakley. 1990. Classification of the Natural Communities of North Carolina Third Approximation. North Carolina Natural Heritage Program Division of Parks and Recreation N.C. Department of Environment, Health and Natural Resources, Raleigh, North Carolina, USA.

Schultz, A. P., and R. R. Seal II. 1997. Geology and geologic history of Great Smoky Mountains National Park; a simple guide for the interpretive program. Open-File Report OF 97-0510. U.S. Geological Survey, Reston, Virginia. USA.

Secor, D. T., Jr., C. A. Barker, M. G. Balinsky, and D. J. Colquhoun. 1998. Pages 1–16 in The Carolina terrane in northeastern South Carolina: History of an exotic volcanic arc. Carolina Geological Society Guidebook for 1998 Annual Meeting. Carolina Geological Society, Durham, North Carolina, USA.

Shafer, D. S. 1986. Flat Laurel Gap Bog, Pisgah Ridge, North Carolina; late Holocene development of a high-elevation heath bald. Castanea 51(1):1–9.

Steichen, P. 1982. Carl Sandburg Home: Carl Sandburg Home National Historic Site, North Carolina. U.S. Department of the Interior, Washington, District of Columbia, USA.

Stover, C. W. and J. L. Coffman. 1993. Seismicity of the United States, 1568-1989 (Revised). Professional Paper 1527. U.S. Geological Survey, Reston, Virginia, USA.

Tull, J. F. and Li, L. 1998. Cover stratigraphy and structure of the southernmost external basement massifs in the Appalachian Blue Ridge; evidence for two-stage Neoproterozoic rifting. Geological Society of America Abstracts with Programs 30(7):124.

Vauchez, A. and M. Brunel, M. 1988. Polygenetic evolution and longitudinal transport within the Henderson mylonitic gneiss, North Carolina (southern Appalachian Piedmont). Geology (Boulder) 16(11):1011–1014.

Wallace, D. H. 1984. Historic Furnishings Report: Main House and Swedish House at Carl Sandburg Home National Historic Site, Flat Rock, North Carolina. NPS Internal document.

Ware, S. and G. Pinion. 1990. Substrate adaptation in rock outcrop plants-eastern United States Talinum (Portulacaceae). Bulletin of the Torrey Botany Club 117:284–290.

White, R. D., Jr. 2003. Vascular plant inventory and plant community classification for Carl Sandburg Home National Historic Site. NatureServe, Durham, North Carolina

Wieczorek, G. F. and B. A. Morgan. 2008. Debris-flow hazards within the Appalachian Mountains of the Eastern United States. Fact Sheet 2008-3070. U.S. Geological Survey, Reston, Virginia, USA. http://pubs.usgs.gov/fs/2008/3070/. Accessed 4 August 2011.

Wieczorek, G. F. and J. B. Snyder. 2009. Monitoring slope movements. Pages 245–271 in R. Young and L. Norby, editors. Geological Monitoring. Geological Society of America, Boulder, Colorado, USA. http://nature.nps.gov/geology/monitoring/slopes.cfm. Accessed 4 August 2011.

Williams, S. T. and Hatcher, R. D., Jr. 2000. Detailed geologic mapping from the western to central Inner Piedmont, North Carolina. Geological Society of America Abstracts with Programs 32:A-83.

Wiser, S. K., P. K. Peet, and P. S. White. 1996. High elevation rock outcrop vegetation of the southern Appalachian Mountains. Journal of Vegetation Science 7:703–722.

Woolsey, J. and G. Walker. 2008. A Vegetational Assessment of the Granitic Rock Outcrop Communities at Carl Sandburg Home National Historic Park. NPS report prepared in cooperation with Appalachian State University.

Yanagihara, G. M. and T. L. Davis. 1992. Relationships between deformation and metamorphism in the western Inner Piedmont, North Carolina. Geological Society of America Abstracts with Programs 24(7):238.

Additional References

This section lists additional references, resources, and web sites that may be of use to resource managers. Web addresses are current as of March 2012.

Geology of National Park Service Areas

National Park Service Geologic Resources Division (Lakewood, Colorado). http://nature.nps.gov/geology/

NPS Geologic Resources Inventory. http://www.nature.nps.gov/geology/inventory/gre_publications.cfm

Harris, A. G., E. Tuttle, and S. D. Tuttle. 2003. Geology of National Parks. Sixth Edition. Kendall/Hunt Publishing Co., Dubuque, Iowa, USA.

Kiver, E. P. and D. V. Harris. 1999. Geology of U.S. parklands. John Wiley and Sons, Inc., New York, New York, USA.

Lillie, R. J. 2005. Parks and Plates: The geology of our national parks, monuments, and seashores. W.W. Norton and Co., New York, New York, USA. [Geared for interpreters].

NPS Geoscientist-in-the-parks (GIP) internship and guest scientist program. http://www.nature.nps.gov/geology/gip/index.cfm

Resource Management/Legislation Documents

NPS 2006 Management Policies (Chapter 4; Natural Resource Management): http://www.nps.gov/policy/mp/policies.html#_Toc157232681

NPS-75: Natural Resource Inventory and Monitoring Guideline: http://www.nature.nps.gov/nps75/nps75.pdf

NPS Natural Resource Management Reference Manual #77: http://www.nature.nps.gov/Rm77/

Geologic Monitoring Manual
R. Young and L. Norby, editors. Geological Monitoring. Geological Society of America, Boulder, Colorado. http://nature.nps.gov/geology/monitoring/index.cfm

NPS Technical Information Center (Denver, repository for technical (TIC) documents): http://etic.nps.gov/

Geological Survey and Society Websites

North Carolina Geological Survey: http://www.geology.enr.state.nc.us/

North Carolina Geological Survey publications: http://www.geology.enr.state.nc.us/bibliogr.htm

U.S. Geological Survey: http://www.usgs.gov/

Geological Society of America: http://www.geosociety.org/

American Geological Institute: http://www.agiweb.org/

Association of American State Geologists: http://www.stategeologists.org/

Other Geology/Resource Management Tools

Neuendorf, K. K. E., J. P. Mehl Jr., and J. A. Jackson. 2005. Glossary of geology. Fifth edition. American Geological Institute, Alexandria, Virginia, USA.

Bates, R. L. and J. A. Jackson, editors. American Geological Institute dictionary of geological terms (3rd Edition). Bantam Doubleday Dell Publishing Group, New York.

U.S. Geological Survey National Geologic Map Database (NGMDB): http://ngmdb.usgs.gov/

U.S. Geological Survey Geologic Names Lexicon (GEOLEX; geologic unit nomenclature and summary): http://ngmdb.usgs.gov/Geolex/geolex_home.html

U.S. Geological Survey Geographic Names Information System (GNIS; search for place names and geographic features, and plot them on topographic maps or aerial photos): http://gnis.usgs.gov/

U.S. Geological Survey GeoPDFs (download searchable PDFs of any topographic map in the United States): http://store.usgs.gov (click on "Map Locator").

U.S. Geological Survey Publications Warehouse (many USGS publications are available online): http://pubs.er.usgs.gov

U.S. Geological Survey, description of physiographic provinces: http://tapestry.usgs.gov/Default.html

Appendix: Scoping Session Participants

The following is a list of participants from the GRI scoping session for Carl Sandburg National Historic Site, held on May 10–12, 2000. The contact information and email addresses in this appendix may be outdated; please contact the Geologic Resources Division for current information. The scoping meeting summary was used as the foundation for this GRI report. The original scoping summary document is available on the GRI publications web site: http://www.nature.nps.gov/geology/inventory/ gre_publications.cfm. A follow-up conference call occurred on May 3, 2011.

2000 Scoping Participants

Name	Affiliation
Joe Gregson	NPS, Natural Resources Information Division
Tim Connors	NPS, Geologic Resources Division
Warren Weber	NPS, Carl Sandburg Home NHS
Bambi Teague	NPS, Blue Ridge Parkway
Mark Carter	Virginia Division of Mineral Resources
Carl Merschat	North Carolina Geologic Survey
Chris Ulrey	NPS, Blue Ridge Parkway
Lindsay McClelland	NPS, Geologic Resources Division
David Anderson	NPS, Blue Ridge Parkway
Scott Southworth	US Geological Survey
Nick Evans	Virginia Division of Mineral Resources

2011 Conference Call Participants

Name	Affiliation
Mark Carter	US Geological Survey
Tim Connors	NPS, Geologic Resources Division
Jeri DeYoung	NPS, Carl Sandburg Home NHS
Jason Kenworthy	NPS, Geologic Resources Division
Philip Reiker	NPS, Geologic Resources Division
Trista Thornberry-Ehrlich	Colorado State University
Irene Van Hoff	NPS, Carl Sandburg Home NHS

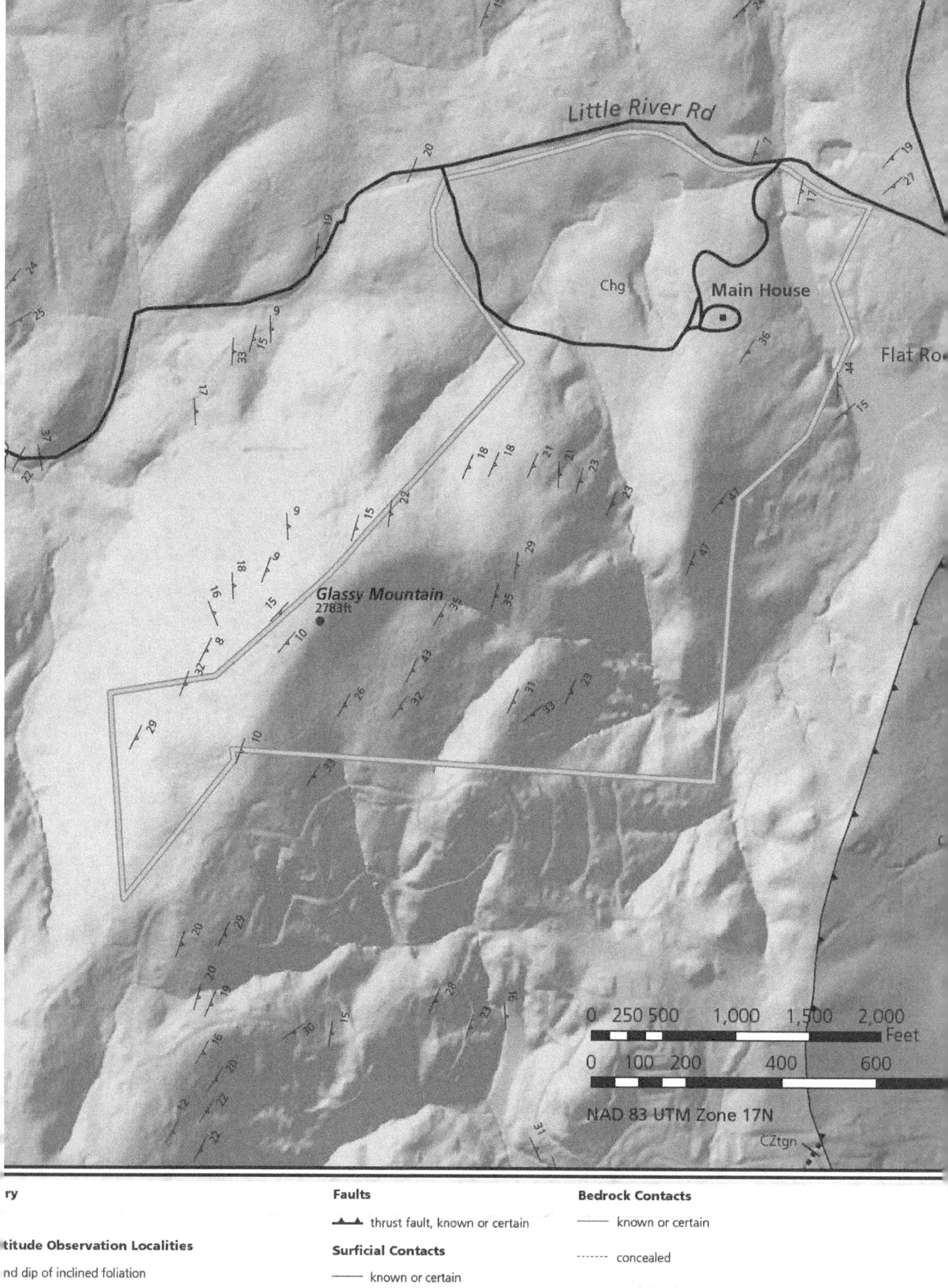

Little River Rd

Chg

Main House

Flat Ro

Glassy Mountain
2783ft

Faults

⊿⊿⊿ thrust fault, known or certain

Surficial Contacts

—— known or certain

Bedrock Contacts

—— known or certain

----- concealed

▪▪▪▪ gradational

ry

titude Observation Localities

nd dip of inclined foliation

0   250 500   1,000   1,500   2,000
Feet

0   100 200   400   600

NAD 83 UTM Zone 17N

CZtgn

Geologic Description	Geologic Issues	Geologic Features and Processes	
...ontains gravel, sand, silt, and clay deposits ...ted with streams and rivers. These deposits are loose, ...solidated sediments and they collect along stream ...ls, in surficial depressions, and on floodplains.	Qal is associated with active stream channels and delicate riparian habitats, and thus should be avoided for most forms of heavy development. Very low erosion resistance. Sedimentation issues associated with streams and ponds in the park, although not mapped in the park.	Unit may contain historic artifacts. Unit contains gravel, sand, silt, and clay resources. Qal is associated with riparian and riverine habitats.	
...vas an igneous (or formerly molten magma) rock that ...n changed by heat and pressure, called ...orphism, into a light-gray, medium-grained rock that ...s striped or banded in appearance, due to alternating ...of light and dark minerals. This unit contains lenses of ...ich gneiss, and is interlayered with Chg, below, ...eastern contact. SOgg may appear as lenses within ...below.	Where unit crops out on sloped areas, blockfall may be a potential hazard. High erosion resistance.	In order of relative abundance, unit contains: plagioclase feldspar, quartz, microcline, biotite, muscovite, sphene, epidote, allanite, zircon, opaque minerals	mapped previously by Kei... metamorphosed during m... events).
...s also a metamorphosed igneous rock that appears ...gray to medium-bluish gray in outcrop exposures. ...it is generally massive, or appears relatively ...enous, with strong foliation defined as alternating ...of dark and light minerals. This banding formed as the ...s exposed to intense heat and pressure. Its ...teristic augen (German word for "eyes") appear as ...of roundish crystals surrounded by swirling bands. ...augen are generally less than 2.5 cm (1 in.) in diameter ...sist of the mineral microcline (a feldspar, see ...ry). Chg is darker than SOgg and contains the ...cuous augen; Chg has a gradational contact with ...below. ...mapped within park boundaries. More recent ...g by the North Carolina Geological Survey ...ned that Chg is the only bedrock unit within the park	Balds may be prone to focusing erosion during runoff events. Where unit crops out on sloped areas, blockfall may be a potential hazard. In areas where people have created social trails to the balds, such as at Little Glassy, foot traffic could dislodge rocks to visitor use areas below. High erosion resistance.	Balds developed on this unit were ceremonial areas for native Cherokee, and trading locales for European settlers. Flat Rock, North Carolina is named for balds or bedrock exposures of Chg. At least nine significant balds occur within the park. Unit contains microcline (feldspar) augen in a matrix of, in order of relative abundance: biotite, muscovite, epidote, allanite, sphene, apatite, zircon, and opaque minerals. Chg is associated with prominent bedrock balds in the park area; these are enigmatic areas below treeline that support only low shrubs and grasses. This type of bedrock does not buffer the pH of acidic meteoric water, and probably contributes to acidic soils. Biodiversity on balds is low compared to surrounding areas.	(1905). mountain building (oroge... enjoyed walking, sitting, a... around him. ...estate Rock Hill. Elliso... Sandburg's) named it Con... landscape along Ireland's
...a medium-gray, medium-grained schistose rock. It ...s flaky and platy in outcrop. This appearance is due to ...allel alignment of flat, mica minerals, such as ...vite and biotite. CZts also has tourmaline crystals ...the aligned micas. The muscovite crystals in this unit is highly ...nd lustrous. When the feldspar crystals in this unit ...lown, they become light brown and impart a spotted ...ance to the outcrop exposure. This unit weathers to a ...brown saprolite with flecks of the lustrous mica.	Due to weathered and schistose (flaky) nature of this unit, it may be unstable on slopes and may provide a slip surface during mass wasting events. Moderate erosion resistance.	Tourmaline may have provided gem material. Unit contains muscovite, biotite, quartz, feldspar, and tourmaline. Unit weathers to produce clay-rich soils.	building (orogenic) events...

Zgms has three rock types grouped into the same d unit on the basis of their proximity and interlayered nships. The three rock types are a schist, amphibolite, eiss. The lustrous, flaky schist appears dark-gray to gray in unweathered exposures. The individual ls are medium-grained. Roundish garnet crystals as bulges between the schistose layers. CZgms also s dark-gray to medium-gray, medium-grained olite. The amphibolite weathers to a brown to brown, clay-rich saprolite. The gneiss is gray to ray and medium-grained. Thin bands of hornblende- ark mineral) layers define its foliation, or banding. g laterally and vertically with the hornblende gneiss is edium-grained, feldspar-rich quartzite, with very lor banding. The mixed gneiss and quartzite are y folded; they appear in weathered outcrop as buff- and yellow-brown rock exposures.	Garnet may have provided abrasive material. Near Mine Gap, a chromium-bearing mineral, fuschite, is present. Unit contains hornblende, muscovite, biotite, quartz, plagioclase feldspar (oligoclase to andesine), microcline feldspar, garnet, and opaque minerals. Rock types weather to produce clay-rich soils.	Due to the weathered and schistose (flaky) nature of the muscovite schist unit, it may be unstable on slopes and provide a slip surface during mass wasting events. Thick saprolite developed on weathered portions of CZgms may hinder drainage. Where unit crops out on sloped areas, blockfall may be a potential hazard. Moderate to high erosion resistance for quartzite-rich gneisses.	to regional metam… mountain-building events
tites like CZtgn are metamorphic rocks that form conditions where the heat and pressure are such that k partially melts and flows. Portions of the original main intact as stringers and boudins (sausage-shaped CZtgn contains large clumps (blasts) of feldspar s that may reach 15 cm (6 in.) in diameter. When weathers, it becomes a thick saprolite with relict rs of CZgms. CZtgn has a gradational contact with d also contains lenses of biotite granitic gneiss that SOgg.	In order of relative abundance, unit contains: quartz, plagioclase feldspar, microcline feldspar, biotite, muscovite, opaque minerals, epidote, chlorite, and zircon. Rock types weather to produce clay-rich soils.	Thick saprolite developed on weathered portions of this unit may hinder drainage. Where unit crops out on sloped areas, blockfall may be a potential hazard. Moderately high erosion resistance.	during burial deep within building events.
extremely fine-grained, so that individual crystals d to discern with the naked eye. Ultramylonite forms eme deformation, at depths where the pressure and ature cause the rocks to "flow" plastically rather than brittly. CZmy weathers to appear blocky, and dark to black in outcrop exposures. is an isolated, linear geologic unit mapped within in the southeast corner of the geologic map.	Ledges of CZmy may have functioned as landmarks. Unit consists of very fine-grained siliceous (containing silica) rocks. Unit forms resistant ledges in streams and may provide riffle habitat for aquatic life.	CZmy forms resistant ledges and breaks apart in blocky masses. Where undercut by erosion, this may cause a blockfall hazard. High erosion resistance.	CZmy records conditions stress deep within the Ear… events.

The Department of the Interior protects and manages the nation's natural resources and cultural heritage; provides scientific and other information about those resources; and honors its special responsibilities to American Indians, Alaska Natives, and affiliated Island Communities.

NPS 445/113350, March 2012

www.ingramcontent.com/pod-product-compliance
Lightning Source LLC
Chambersburg PA
CBHW080910290526

45795CB00007BA/2477